Best Walks in Buckinghamshire

by Bus and Train

Edited by Barry Totterdell

Buckinghamshire and
West Middlesex Area
of the Ramblers' Association

Published 1998
by Buckinghamshire and West Middlesex Area
of the Ramblers' Association
15 Bowlers Orchard
Chalfont St Giles,
Bucks, HP8 4LB

ISBN 1 901184 11 0

British Library Cataloguing-in-Publication Data
A catalogue record for this book is available from the British Library

Any surplus from the sale of this book will be employed in furthering the
charitable aims of the Ramblers' Association.

Produced by Axxent Ltd
The Old Council Offices
The Green
Datchet
Berkshire, SL3 9EH

Cover photograph
by
Barry Totterdell

INTRODUCTION

Why this book?

In September 1995 the Ramblers' Association celebrated its Jubilee – 60 years of working for walkers! The Buckinghamshire and West Middlesex Area launched its Jubilee campaign at that time, to persuade people walking in the Bucks countryside to leave their cars at home. We felt that, as an organisation which cared about the countryside, it was our duty to try and avoid adding to the pollution, noise and congestion caused by traffic in the country. As part of the campaign, it was agreed that we should publish this book, giving some examples of enjoyable walks in beautiful countryside which could be reached easily by public transport. In many ways, completing a "linear" walk can be more satisfying, and give a greater sense of achievement than doing a circular one, which brings you back to where you started.

A combined effort.

A lot of experience, thought and effort has gone into the book by quite a few people, helped by being able to drawn on the experience of the authors of our last publication *The Vale of Aylesbury Walker* – Peter and Diana Gulland. The walks were originally suggested and then written up by Tom Berry, Clive Bostle, John Esslemont, Ed Kendrick, Grace Miles, Jim Rodda, Brian Shelley and Barry Totterdell. The route descriptions were tested, checked and re-checked by (variously) Paul Alexander, Clive Bostle, David Bradnack and Brian Shelley. Alan and Jean Kelly acted as consumer guinea pigs by testing some of the walk descriptions in their final form. As Editor, Barry Totterdell checked all the walks (most of them twice) and made the final decision on the exact routes and the wording. He also researched and wrote the background information on places of interest, and accepts full responsibility for any errors. Final checking of the text was carried out by David Bradnack.

The maps were a joint effort by Barry Totterdell and David Bradnack. We would like to thank Stephen Forster for his practical assistance, Thames Valley Orienteering Club for letting us use their copy of OCAD6 for drawing the maps in their final form, John Farren for advice about the programme, and Katy Phipps and her family for the use of their computer and for technical support.

Getting there

All of the walks in this book have been chosen for their accessibility by good public transport services. Recent drastic reductions in Sunday bus services, however, make it particularly important that you check in advance if you plan to travel on that day.

> Buckinghamshire County Council runs a *TraveLine* enquiry service, with full information on all bus and train services, on 0345 382000 from 7 am to 8 pm (from 8 am on weekends and bank holidays). Details may also be found in the Travel Guides published by the County Council and available from libraries, tourist information centres, bus and railway stations and some newsagents, and on the World Wide Web at http://www.buckscc.gov.uk/travel info

A word about maps

If we have done our job properly, you shouldn't need maps – the route descriptions alone should enable you to follow the walks without getting lost. We have, however, included a map for each of the 16 walks, for interest rather than detailed guidance. Many walkers, though, like to have a detailed map for the full picture. There is only one map series we can recommend for this – the Ordnance Survey Pathfinder and Explorer maps at a scale of 1:25000, or about 2½ inches to the mile. As we went to press the Pathfinders were in the process of being replaced by Explorers. These are astonishing value for money, with more information, and covering a much larger area, than earlier maps – some are even double sided. Already, the two maps covering the Chiltern Hills (North and South) take in 11 of the walks in this book completely. For Walk 15 we recommend the official city map of Milton Keynes.

A warning

Any book of walks is inevitably out of date almost as soon as it's published. Stiles are replaced by kissing gates, hedges and fences are removed, fields which have been pasture for many years are ploughed up, buildings are demolished, and new houses erected. All of the walks had a final check only a week or so before the manuscript was delivered to our printers, and we have, in any case, tried as far as possible to use relatively permanent features where directions are critical.

Refreshments

We have given information about pubs, cafés and restaurants, but these, too, change over the years. Three pubs closed while the book was in preparation, but one of these reopened under new management and another was transformed into a "diner" just before we went to press. Pubs in isolated situations or the smaller villages are shown on the maps by "PH". It wasn't feasible to show these individually in the towns and larger villages. Landlords are understandably unhappy about muddy boots in their bars, or customers eating their own sandwiches.

Points of interest

We hope you find the background information about the places visited and the people connected with them interesting. Churches are marked on the maps by a +. When we asked about churches which were closed, we were told: "Oh, you dare not leave them unlocked these days", although in fact we found nearly two thirds of them open. We have generally given opening hours of historic houses and other buildings open to the public, in general terms; these may change in detail over the years.

What to wear

For several walks we give warnings about mud. In reality, you will find muddy stretches on most of the walks in wet winter weather. In these conditions you really need hiking boots. Otherwise stout shoes will suffice, or even – in very dry weather – trainers. Walk 15 is different: it's all on made-up surfaces, and no special footwear is needed at any time of year. Clothing is a matter of common sense, though be warned – the wind can be biting on the Chilterns ridge in winter!

Where next?

There is an increasing choice of walks in this area which make use of bus and train services. *The Thames Path* (Official Guide by David Sharp) is easily accessed by public transport. The East Berkshire Group of the Ramblers' Association have published a book in their *Rambling for Pleasure* series on the *Thames Valley and Chilterns* which is planned to exploit the good local bus and train network. Thames Trains offer a Thames Path Ticket which enables you to travel to one station and return from another at the cost of a cheap day return.

Bucks County Council has promoted a number of linear walks which are well served by buses and trains. *The South Bucks Way*, from Coombe Hill near Wendover to the Grand Union Canal at Denham, shadows public transport routes for much of the way. *The Two Ridges Walk* is followed by our Walk 12. *The Chess Valley Walk* can be reached from Underground stations at Chesham, Chalfont and Latimer, Chorleywood and Rickmansworth. *The Aylesbury Ring*, (devised by John Maples and Ray Knowles of the Ramblers' Association's Aylesbury Group), is a circular walk of 31 miles around Aylesbury which intersects bus or train routes at frequent intervals. Leaflets on these and other Bucks County Council walks can be obtained – for a small charge – from libraries, tourist information centres or the Countryside Service, Environmental Services Department, County Hall, Aylesbury.

The Groundwork Trust have issued a series of leaflets under the title *Ramble and Ride* about walks between railway stations in the Colne Valley (available from stations or from the Trust at the Colne Valley Park Centre, Denham).

The Ramblers' Association

The Ramblers' Association exists to facilitate, for the benefit of everyone, the enjoyment and discovery on foot of Britain's countryside, and to foster a greater knowledge, love and care of the countryside. It works for the preservation of natural beauty and the protection of rights of way, and campaigns for freedom to roam over open country. Local groups organise full programmes of walks, and volunteers alert highway authorities to obstructions and other problems, and help to keep paths open.

If you join us, you will be supporting the work that the Association does. You will also receive *Rambling Today*, the quarterly magazine, and will be put in touch with your local group. For further details contact the Ramblers' Association, 1/5 Wandsworth Road, London, SW8 2XX (telephone 0171-339 8500)

INTRODUCTION

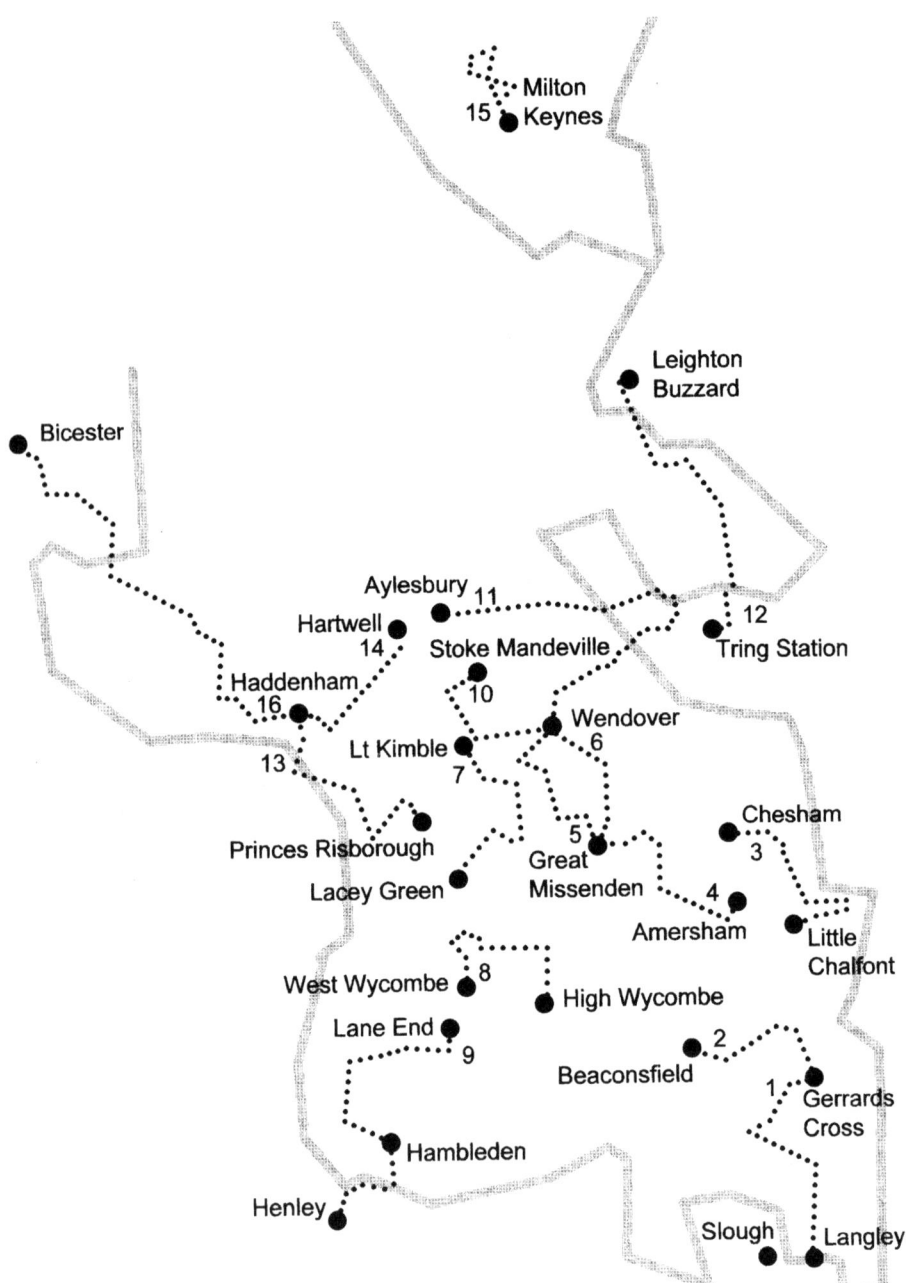

THE WALKS

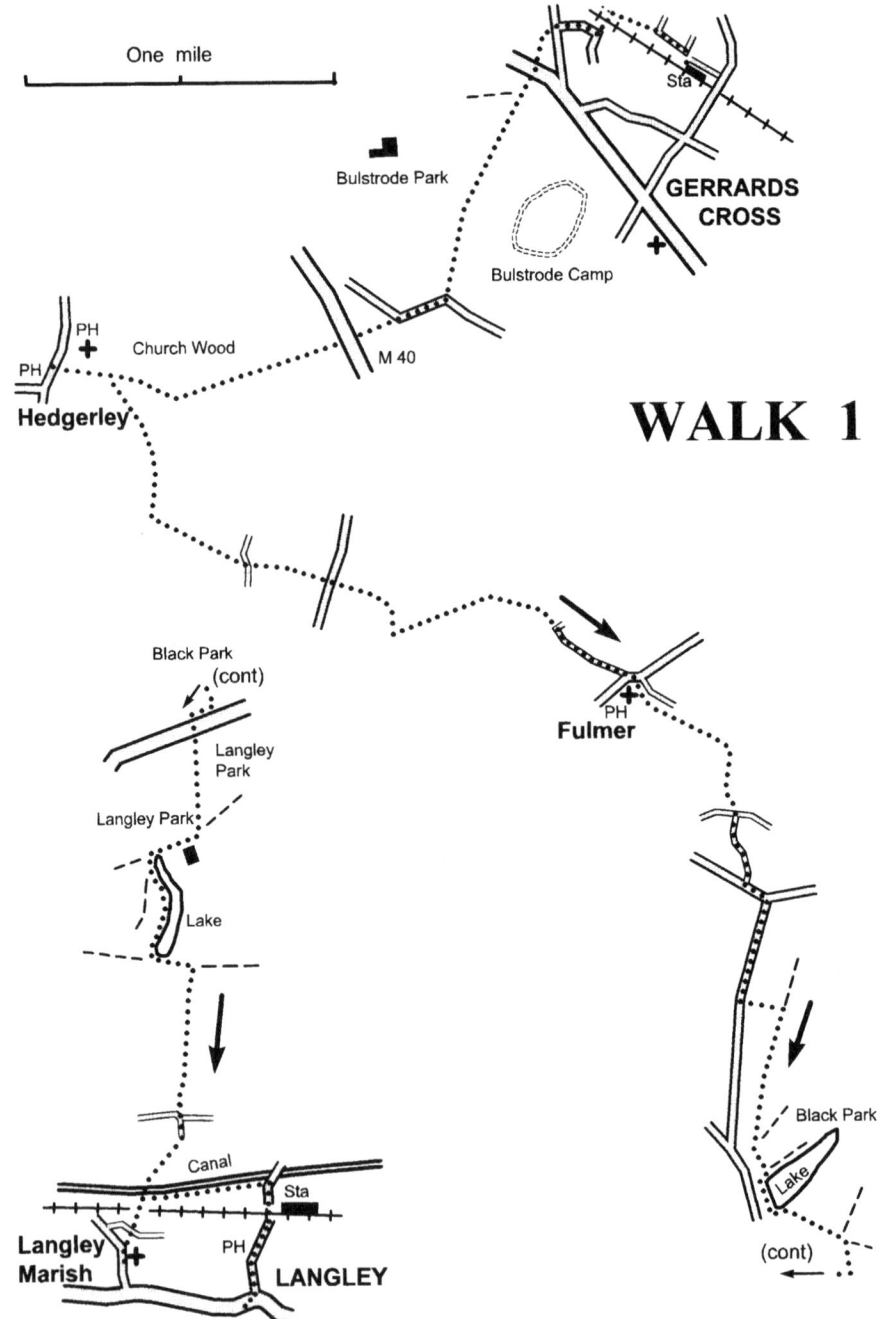

One mile

Bulstrode Park

GERRARDS CROSS ✝

Sta

Bulstrode Camp

PH ✝ Church Wood

PH

Hedgerley M 40

WALK 1

Black Park
(cont)

Langley
Park

Langley Park

Lake

Fulmer PH ✝

Black Park

Lake

(cont)

Canal

Sta

**Langley
Marish** ✝ PH **LANGLEY**

WALK 1: GERRARDS CROSS TO LANGLEY

This walk strings together some of the best walking near to West London – old villages, churches, pubs, nature reserves and country parks – even a canal. In fact, something for everyone!

10 miles

Travel

Gerrards Cross is on the Chiltern Line between Marylebone and High Wycombe, with a frequent service. Langley is also well served by trains on the Paddington, Slough and Reading line. Buses link Gerrards Cross with Uxbridge, Amersham and Slough (not Sundays), and Langley with Uxbridge and Slough. There is a bus service (not Sundays) from Langley to Beaconsfield and High Wycombe.

Refreshments

Gerrards Cross has a choice of pubs, restaurants and cafes; there are pubs at Hedgerley, Fulmer and Langley. When we went to press, the refreshment hut in Black Park was closed, but you should find a mobile snack bar in the car park.

Route

Gerrards Cross is named after the crossroads on the old road from London to Oxford. It was an insignificant hamlet until Victorian times, when it was described as a "highly respectable place with many genteel residences". Not that many, in fact, until the opening of the joint Great Western and Great Central Railway station in 1906. A brochure published in 1917 praised its advantages for commuters: "The inadequate, congested and unpunctual service which marks so many of the suburban lines is here unknown". Gerrards Cross grew rapidly from then on, but has always maintained its affluent air, with a large number of substantial villas. Across the common just to the south of the town and adjoining the A40 is St James's Church, an unlikely building in the Byzantine style built in 1859 by Sir William Tite, the architect of the Royal Exchange. *The church is staffed on Monday to Friday: to view the interior ring the office bell in the east wall.*

The walk starts from Gerrards Cross Station. Cross from the station building by the zebra crossing and take the path opposite which goes up the hill to the left. This leads to Orchehill Rise. Go along this road and where it turns right go straight ahead along a narrow path. After 200 yards turn left and cross the railway by a footbridge. At a road turn right and follow this downhill to Bull Lane. Cross, and go along a narrow signposted path, alongside a fence, through a small copse and up steps to the busy A40. Cross this with care, go 25 yards to the left, and down a path on the right. Follow this to a wide drive and turn right to a kissing gate. Enter Bulstrode Park and follow a clear path to the left along the bottom of the valley.

The history of the Bulstrode Estate goes back to Saxon times. At one time it was owned by the notorious Judge Jeffreys who presided over the Bloody Assizes of 1685, followed by the first Earl of Portland. The house reached its zenith in the mid 18th century, when the then Duchess of Portland made it an artistic centre. Among its treasures at the time was the famous Portland Vase, now in the British Museum. The present house, which was built in 1862, can be glimpsed over to the right among the trees. It is now the headquarters of the Worldwide Evangelization Crusade. *Permission to view the gardens, with their lovely trees and shrubs, landscaped walks and ponds, can be obtained by asking at reception in the main house.*

Across to the left is Bulstrode Camp, the largest Iron Age hillfort in Buckinghamshire, now surrounded by houses.

The path continues over a stile, and eventually joins a track from the right and goes through a kissing gate. Here go straight ahead along a wider stony track and through a gateway at the end. Go past the entrance to "Ponders" bearing right along Hedgerley Lane. At the first bend go straight ahead on a footpath which goes over a stile by a gate, under the M40 and on through a kissing gate and along a field edge to a stile. Cross this and continue in the same direction through the next three fields, keeping just to the left of Church Wood when you reach it.

Just before the end of the third field there is a kissing gate on the right into Church Wood nature reserve. The reserve is a long-

established one, owned by the Royal Society for the Protection of Birds. It is freely open to the public.

Our route goes ahead, over a stile, and along an enclosed track into Hedgerley village.

The village used to be famous for its bricks, and this is reflected in many of the attractive buildings and the name of one of the two pubs. The Old Quaker House, just up the road from the White Hart, was the scene of a famous, then illegal, meeting in 1666 of Quakers, which was broken up by the authorities. The church is by Benjamin Ferrey, who designed the present Bulstrode House. It contains a fragment of velvet said to be a piece of Charles I's cloak, which he left as a covering for the altar when calling at the church while on a hunting expedition. A 17th century painting of the ten commandments is also worth seeing. *The church is open from Easter to the end of September on Sunday afternoons.* **A permissive path leads direct from the churchyard back down to the track by which we entered the village.**

On leaving Hedgerley retrace your steps along the enclosed track to the stile at the end and go diagonally right across a large field to a stile on the edge of a wood. Follow the path up through the wood and ahead along the edge of a field to a copse. Go over a footbridge and stile and turn left. Follow the fenced track along the edge of the field, cross a stile, then go slightly right across a field aiming for another stile at the left-hand end of a large group of farm buildings. Cross the stile, and go straight ahead with the farmyard on your right, across a track and bear right to a stile by an enormous redwood tree. Cross the next field half right to a further stile with a small footbridge, then still in the same direction to a stile in the hedge. Climb this and drop down to a lane. Cross the lane and go up a stony track to Tara Stud. Look for, and follow, a path to the right of the entrance. Follow this to a stile, then on along the field edge to cross yet another stile and emerge onto the B416 Windsor Road.

Cross the road, with care, to a stile almost opposite. Once over this follow the path ahead through an area which has been worked for sand and gravel for years. The path eventually bends right, past some large oak trees, towards a group of old buildings – "The Pickeridge". Cross a wide concrete road (former access to quarry plant) and bear left to walk along a wide grassy track. Follow it downhill, between quarry plant and The Pickeridge, to a gate and stile. Continue on to the corner of the field. Go through a kissing gate, over a footbridge, and along a narrow field to another kissing gate. Pass through this and continue on, with views to the left of water meadows and lakes (and, unfortunately, the M40) to a kissing gate into Hay Lane. Follow this ahead, passing the imposing Fulmer Hall on the right, to reach Fulmer.

Fulmer, which means lake of birds, takes its name from a large marshy area, the remnants of which you passed a quarter of a mile back. Cress was grown there in the 19th century. The village itself is modest, but its situation in pleasant countryside so near to London led to the building of a number of imposing country houses on its periphery in the 18th and 19th centuries. The church was rebuilt in 1610 by Sir Marmaduke Dayrell, Master of the King's Household, whose impressive monument is inside, together with the story of his life.

From Hay Lane, cross Windmill Road and follow the churchyard wall to the left. Just before Alderbourne Lane, turn right along the drive to Muschamp Stud and Church Farm. When the drive bears right continue ahead alongside the Alderbourne to a kissing gate. Go through, and head slightly right to a stile at the far end of the field, by a white gate and a large oak tree. Continue in roughly the same direction to a kissing gate in the hedge on the right. Go through and follow a clear path uphill across the next field to a gate and a signpost. Continue along the same path, now enclosed, which joins a drive and shortly crosses a private road. In another 50 yards turn right along another private road to reach Fulmer Common Road in a quarter of a mile.

Cross with care, and follow this road to the left for 100 yards, then turn right down Black Park Road. In a quarter of a mile, after the first (slight) bend, go left over a stile by a gate. Follow the path through trees to a stile. You are now in Black Park.

Black Park was originally the northern portion of Langley Park, and was planted with firs in the second part of the 18th century by the then Duke of Marlborough. It's now a country park with a nature reserve, picnic site and a variety of walks and trails.

Go over the stile and turn right along a wide track. This is a bridleway for horses, so keep dogs under close control. Follow the track for half a mile to the car park, ignoring paths and tracks to the left. Cross the car park to the lake and follow the embankment to the right and round the end of the lake, past the toilets and tea hut to the visitor centre (also with toilets). Immediately after the centre turn right, then bear left to join a partly asphalted track. At the second "crossroads", where there are picnic tables, turn right, soon passing estate houses to reach the extremely busy – and fast – A412. To cross, go to the right, to where you can see round the bend, then cross this dual carriageway, very carefully. Opposite is the main entrance to Langley Park.

Ignore off-putting signs and follow the drive as far as the wrought iron gates which mark the entrance to Langley Park House.

> **The house was built by the 3rd Duke of Marlborough in 1755/58 as a hunting lodge, and includes a range of interesting outbuildings. The park is owned by the County Council and is freely open all the year round. It includes a lovely lake, an arboretum, an area of azaleas and rhododendrons, and extensive open space and woodland.**

Turn right here and follow the track to a gate near one end of the lake. Go through and walk along near the shore of the lake, with splendid views now of the house. At the far end of the lake go ahead to a broad track behind a raised bank. Turn left, and in 200 yards go through a kissing gate, cross a small stream, then turn right through a gap by a stile. Follow the path across a field towards a belt of trees. Go through these, over a stile and across another field to another stile. Cross this and follow a short path to a road, part of Trenches Farm Estate. Go along Blenheim Close ahead. Between nos. 14 and 15 go down a path, across a children's play area, over a footbridge and along a path to a canal. Cross the canal bridge.

If you are not too tired, and not rushing to catch a bus or train, it would be a shame to miss Old Langley, or more correctly, Langley Marish. After crossing the canal, continue over the railway and on down to a road . Go across a small green and ahead along a narrow fenced path to arrive near the almshouses, church and two pubs.

> **Surrounded by a large housing estate is the church of St Mary the Virgin. It includes a range of architectural styles, and many features of interest. The greatest is the Kederminster Library, which dates from 1623, said to have been used by John Milton while living nearby. It still houses many ancient and valuable books, but the room itself and its decoration is pretty amazing.** *The church and the library are unfortunately only open on the afternoon of the first Sunday in June, July, August and September.*
>
> **The smaller group of almshouses was founded in 1617 by Sir John Kederminster, the Lord of the Manor before the Duke of**

Marlborough, in 1617. The other almshouses date from 1679. Langley Marish used to be part of Buckinghamshire, but is now swallowed up by Slough and assigned to Berkshire. The name "Marish" is nothing to do with a marsh but reflects the Mariscos, early lords of the Manor.

If you are returning to Slough, some buses go from the stop at the end of the road, on the other side of Langley Road. Otherwise, to finish the walk, retrace your steps to the canal, go down to the towpath and turn right – away from the bridge – and follow the canal for half a mile to the next bridge.

The Slough arm of the Grand Union Canal was opened in 1883, and was thus one of the last stretches of canal to be built in Britain. Originally built to carry bricks from the Langley brickfields, it's now used for leisure boating, and provides a 5 mile lock-free route almost in a straight line from Cowley to the centre of Slough. It also makes for a pleasant 5 mile walk or cycle ride.

Leave the canal by going up steps, and turn right into Langley Park Road. The station is on the left in a short distance. The bus stop for Uxbridge is under the railway bridge and on the right past the pub. For buses to Slough continue for a further 100 yards to the next road junction. The bus stop is in Langley Road to the right.

WALK 2: BEACONSFIELD TO GERRARDS CROSS

A civilised walk from the pleasant town of Beaconsfield over a golf course, through unspoilt Seer Green and the unique tranquillity and peace of Jordans, to affluent Gerrards Cross.

6 miles

Travel

Beaconsfield and Gerrards Cross are served by frequent trains between Marylebone and High Wycombe, and on to Aylesbury or Banbury and the Midlands. Beaconsfield is reached by bus from Amersham and Slough (not Sundays), High Wycombe and Uxbridge. Gerrards Cross has bus services from Chesham and Amersham (not Sundays), Slough and Uxbridge.

Refreshments

You are spoilt for choice on this walk. Beaconsfield has a wide range of restaurants, tea shops and pubs in the Old and New Towns, there are two pubs at Seer Green, Old Jordans Guest House is generally open for morning coffee, lunch and afternoon tea, and Gerrards Cross is well served by restaurants, cafes and pubs.

Route

This end of Beaconsfield – the New Town – only really developed following the coming of the railway in 1906. The picturesque Old Town is nearly a mile away to the south, and is built around crossroads (now a roundabout) on the old London to Oxford road. The four roads which radiate from here are lined with a wealth of houses in many styles dating back to the early 17th century, and are called respectively London End, Windsor End, Wycombe End and Aylesbury End. Every Tuesday a popular market is held in Windsor End, and all four Ends are closed on one day each year for the fair. Both fair and market were founded over 700 years ago.

Few small towns can have as many literary associations as Beaconsfield. Edmund Waller, the Civil War poet who was born at Coleshill, built Hall Barn, now the other side of the M40, in

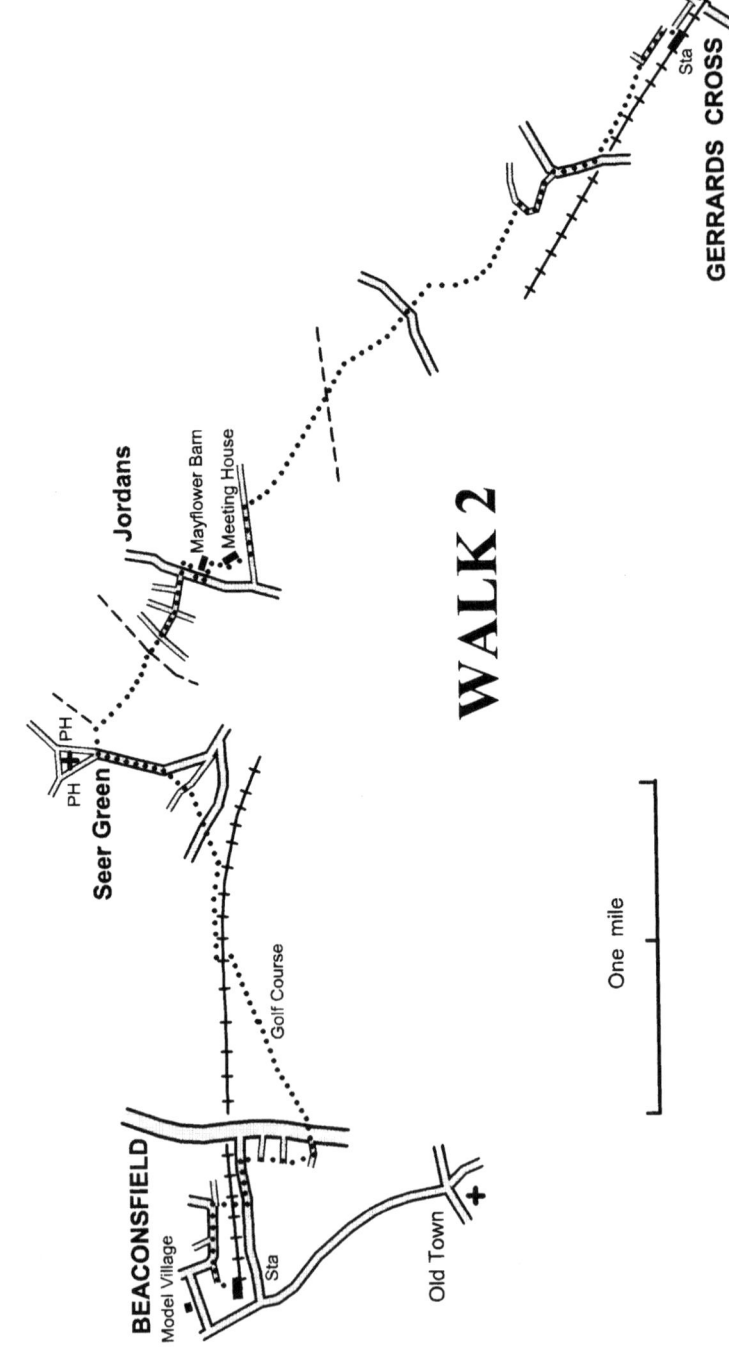

WALK 2

One mile

about 1660. The estate was subsequently acquired by the first Lord Burnham, the newspaper magnate, and has been in the family since. Edmund Burke bought Gregories Estate in 1768 and lived there until his death in 1797. He is buried in the parish church, and the house and estate no longer exist. GK Chesterton lived in Beaconsfield from 1909 until his death in 1936, and the house he had built in Grove Road called "Top Meadow" still stands. He was a well known figure about the town and a bust of him stood for many years in his favourite bar in the White Hart. His grave is in the Roman Catholic cemetery in Shepherds Lane, marked by a headstone carved by Eric Gill.

The American poet Robert Frost brought his young family to Beaconsfield in 1912, and had his first book published while he was living at 26 Reynolds Road. The family used to enjoy walking in the local countryside. Alison Uttley wrote her much loved stories for children about Little Grey Rabbit, Sam Pig and many other animal characters, in the years from 1930 that she was living at "Thackers" in Ellwood Road. Finally, one of the most popular, and certainly most prolific of children's writers, Enid Blyton, had her house "Green Hedges" in Penn Road. The house and garden are no more, having been sold for building, but she is commemorated in the name of the cul-de-sac built on the site – "Blyton Close".

The walk starts from Beaconsfield Station, on the car park side. (If arriving by bus, get off in Maxwell Road, near Sainsburys, and you can simply walk down it away from the town centre, to pick up the walk in a quarter of a mile). From the station building cross the access road and go up a path signposted "Model Village". This leads to Caledon Close, and when you reach it go ahead along Caledon Road.

Bekonscot (left, and left again from here) claims to be the oldest model village in the world. First opened in 1929, it covers one and a half acres, and includes a quarter of a mile of railway track, a third of a mile of roadway, 160 buildings (including a model of "Green Hedges") and some 8000 plants, concentrating on miniature varieties. All the profits go to the Church Army. *Open daily, March to October.*

In a few hundred yards, as Caledon Road becomes One Tree Lane, turn right down a path, over the railway, and onto Maxwell Road. Cross and go left, past St Mary and All Saints School, then the Curzon Centre, then shortly at a public footpath sign turn right along a wide path between houses. Follow this, crossing the ends of two cul-de-sacs, then forking first left, to reach the next road (Ronald Road). Here turn left to the busy Amersham Road. Cross with great care, using the pedestrian refuge, to a signposted footpath opposite. Follow the path diagonally left over the field towards trees. Go through a kissing gate and continue in the same direction passing warning signs for the golf course ahead. It's a good wide path signposted with green and white posts, that sometimes crosses fairways, and bears left after about a third of a mile to cross a railway bridge. Turn right alongside the fence and after a quarter of a mile, at a signpost, go diagonally downhill across the fairways and through a small belt of trees to a stile hidden in trees beyond. Cross the stile to reach Longbottom Lane.

Cross the lane and go up a footpath just a little to the right. In 200 yards, when it joins another path, bear left and go uphill, cross Long Grove and go along a path between hedges to join Vicarage Close for a few yards. Turn left onto the main road, past Seer Green School entrance and the small recreation ground, towards the centre of Seer Green village, reaching the small church hall on the left in 200 yards

> **The village centre is straight ahead, with its two pubs and a mixture of small brick cottages and modern houses. The small church was built in 1847 when Seer Green became a separate parish.**

Opposite the church hall is a track with a footpath sign. Take this, bearing right in 100 yards and follow the track all the way to Jordans, crossing a bridle path at the bottom of the valley on the way. Continue in the same direction on a road which passes the end of Jordans village green.

> **Jordans Village was established by local Quakers in 1919 as a model village, and designed by Fred Rowntree. A plaque on the small building by the green, which houses the offices of Jordans Village Ltd, commemorates Fred Hancock, the first Secretary, and refers to the ideals of the founders that it "should be a community where people of varied beliefs and interests might live and work happily together". Cricket is played on the green in summer and the village store and post office is owned by the community.**

At a T-junction cross over and immediately turn right along a footpath on the other side of the hedge. When the path turns away to the left, emerge back onto the road and across the front of Old Jordans Guest House and its conference centre.

The guest house was originally Jordans Farm. It was acquired in 1639 by William Russell, one of the early Quakers, and served from 1659 as a meeting place of local Quakers. George Fox, who founded the movement, and William Penn worshipped there regularly. Meetings were frequently broken up by the authorities, and worshippers imprisoned. The building was bought by local Friends Meetings in 1911 and developed as a centre for peace and relaxation open to all.

Turn left at the end of the main buildings and go into a car park. The large barn on the left is the Mayflower Barn.

The barn is so called because it is said to have been built from the timbers of the Mayflower in which the Pilgrim Fathers sailed. An eminent antiquarian, Rendel Harris, published a book in 1920 setting out the evidence. Most of this is circumstantial, but it does at the very least add up to a string of quite remarkable coincidences. It certainly was common for redundant sailing vessels to be brought up the Thames and broken up for building, and it is said that if you stand in the barn and look between your legs at the roof, it looks very much like the hold of a wooden sailing ship! *The entrance to the barn is on the other side. If closed, the key may be obtained from the guest house.*

Past the end of the barn, go through a small gate on the right and follow a path down through the simple Quaker burial ground to the front of the Friends Meeting House.

On the right are the graves of William Penn, the founder of Pennsylvania, his wives Gulielma and Hannah, and ten of their 16 children. The simple meeting house, probably the most famous in the country, was built in 1688, the year that the Declaration of Indulgence gave freedom of religion. *Open every day except Monday and Tuesday, but closed at lunch times.*

Leave by the gate near the meeting house and turn left up Welders Lane, soon passing Jordans Youth Hostel. Take care as the road is narrow and can be busy. Walk as far as Welders House, a further 250 yards. Turn right here, over a stile and down a path, which follows a more or less straight line for nearly a mile to Layters Green Lane. After crossing a stile 250 yards from Welders Lane and passing under overhead power cables, you will reach an open field. Cross this, following low electric cables and making for the second double electricity pole at the edge of a wood. Our path goes just to the right of the poles and continues in the same direction into the woods, marked very occasionally by yellow arrows. After about 250 yards you will come to the corner of a field. Take the path which goes slightly to your right and walk along the edge of the wood, with the fence on your left. The path enters woodland again, now with fences on both sides, passing through a kissing gate and soon becoming a track, to reach Layters Green Lane.

Turn left, and almost immediately cross and go down a path on the right. This soon leads to a kissing gate and a path crossing. Go straight on, heading to the right of some large barns which soon become visible, and join a tarmac drive. At first, cross the drive and follow a path on the left behind trees. Soon rejoin the drive and follow it for 300 yards until a path bears off to the left. Go through the kissing gate and follow the path to Maltmans Lane. Turn right, past Oak Manor, and right again at a pillar box into Bull Lane. Immediately before a railway bridge go left along a path parallel with the railway line until it joins a road. At the end of the road, continue on the path which goes down and to the right to Gerrards Cross Station.

WALK 3: CHESHAM TO LITTLE CHALFONT

This walk rises immediately out from Chesham onto the Chiltern plateau, dipping into some delightful dry valleys and passing through the villages of Tylers Hill, Ley Hill and Latimer. It then drops down into the lovely Chess Valley, up the other side to Chenies and its Tudor manor, and along a scenic path above the valley to reach Little Chalfont. The bridleways through the woods near the end can be muddy in winter.

8 miles

Travel

Chesham Station is served by a short shuttle service from Chalfont and Latimer, which is on the London Underground Metropolitan line from central London, and the Chiltern line between Marylebone and Aylesbury via Amersham. Chesham is also linked by bus with Amersham, High Wycombe, Slough, Berkhamsted, Hemel Hempstead and Watford. Little Chalfont is on the bus route between Watford and Chesham, but only the service between Chesham, Amersham and High Wycombe runs on Sundays.

Refreshments

There are pubs and cafés at Chesham and Little Chalfont, and pubs in Tylers Hill and Ley Hill. The Bedford Arms at Chenies is 200 yards along the Chorleywood Road from Chenies village green. The farm shop at Chenies Bottom sells ice cream and soft drinks. Teas are available at Chenies Manor on opening days.

Route

The walk starts from Chesham Station.

The railway line to Chesham was opened in 1889, and was for a few years the terminus of the Metropolitan Railway out of London, before being relegated to branch line status. The well preserved station with its attractive sunken garden is more like a country station than a part of the London Underground.

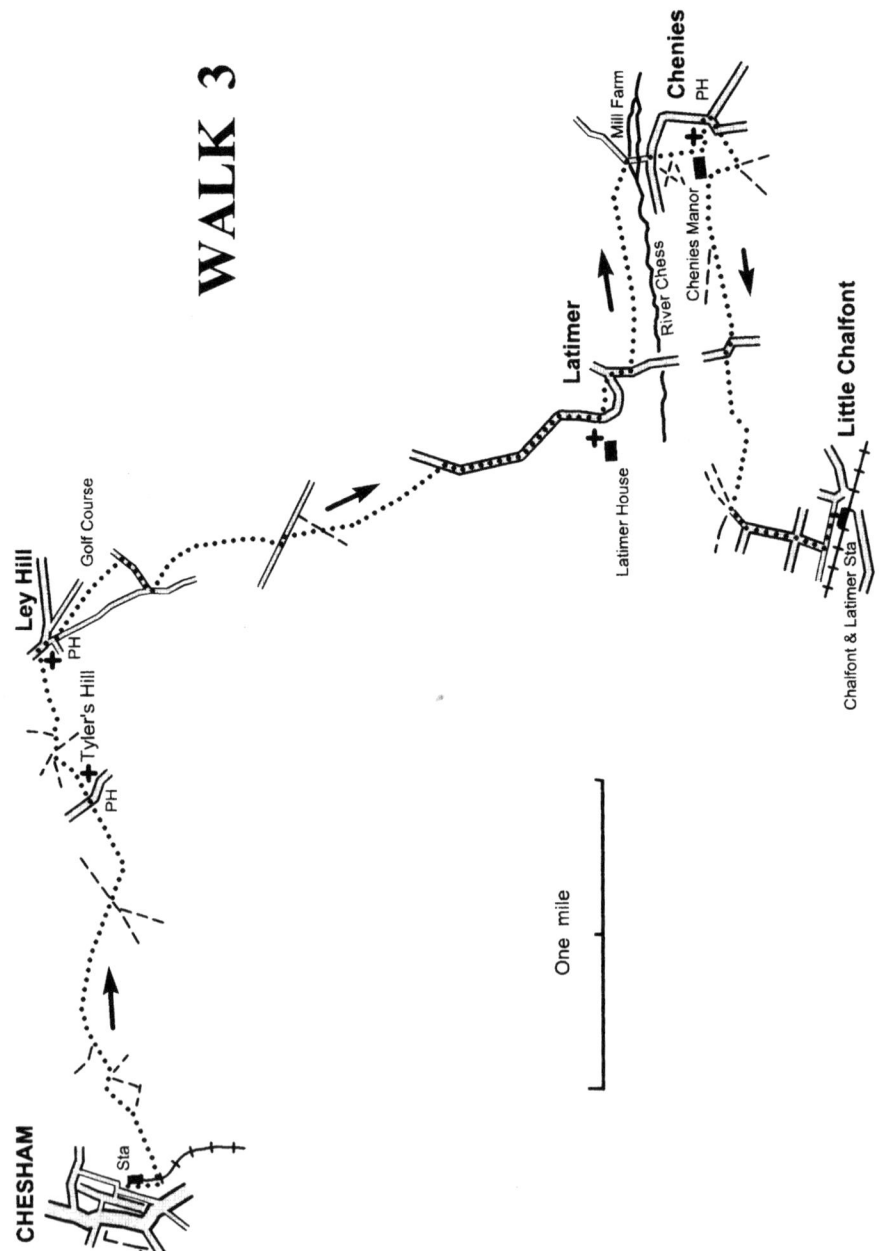

Chesham is rather a workaday town, and was, indeed, very much a manufacturing centre in the 19th century, known locally for the "four bs" – beer, boots, brushes and Baptists (for it was a stronghold of nonconformity). Arthur Liberty, who had a small draper's shop in the High Street, went on to found one of London's most famous stores. The town does have some very attractive features, however. The oldest part, centred on Church Street on the other side of the ring road, has a wealth of attractive buildings near the young River Chess, including The Bury, built in 1712 for William Lowndes, Secretary to the Treasury. The fine Parish Church is nearby, and also Lowndes Park, a magnificent open space which leads westwards to open country and the Chilterns. Our route, which also leads quickly out of the town, is to the east.

From the station turn sharp left, go down steps and take a footpath to the left. After 200 yards, cross the railway by a bridge on the left, turn right, then double back to the left alongside railings. Turn right again up a steep path through the woods, which continues as a hollow way. At the top, cross two stiles, then look back down into the Chess Valley and the rooftops of Chesham.

Continue straight ahead across the field, cross the stile and turn left, to walk along the edge of the next field with the hedge on your left. At the end of this field, cross the stile, turn right and walk along the track for some 100 yards. Dungrove Farm is on your right, but here you climb the stile on your left, and go across the field and over a stile just to the right of some houses. Cross the track and continue ahead by a hedge bordering the back gardens of houses, then the playing fields of Chesham Leisure Centre. The path bends round to the right alongside a tall hedge. Continue into the field ahead and go straight across it to a stile. Cross this, and go down the steep slope in the same direction into the dry valley to the next stile. At the bottom, cross the track and climb up the other side with the hedge on your left, noting the extensive views across to the Chess valley as you reach the top. At the next hedge, turn left, and walk along beside it to the next stile. Cross this and walk across the next field, aiming for the stile just to the left of the white painted Five Bells pub at Tylers Hill.

Cross over the road and walk between Chantry Cottage and the graveyard, cross a stile and walk alongside the edge of the wood. At the field corner in 300 yards, go over a stile to enter the wood. Follow the path to the right and left and between depressions, keeping fairly near the edge of the wood. At a path junction, some 200 yards after entering the wood, turn right by a small pond. In another 100 yards (ignoring a cross-path on the way) go left, keeping the edge of the wood on your left. At the end, leave the woods by a stile, and continue ahead across the left-hand side of the field, alongside the hedge. Cross the stile at the end and walk beside a garden, past the end of a cul-de-sac and then more gardens, to emerge between the Memorial Hall and the Methodist Chapel. Turn right, and bear slightly left to cross a corner of the common and reach Ley Hill's two pubs.

Cross the road to a footpath sign 70 yards past the Swan, by the side of the golf course. Follow the direction shown by the sign, keeping the bushes and trees on your right. Carry on ahead, taking care as you cross a fairway on the next part of the golf course. On reaching a road near the Old School House, turn right and walk down the hill through woods. After 300 yards turn left at a T-junction, and immediately left again over a stile, and follow the left-hand side of this large field alongside a strip of woodland, eventually going down into a dip, then uphill to cross a stile. Cross another stile immediately on your left and continue in the same direction through a small wood. Leave the wood in 50 yards, and keeping the hedge on your right, walk on until you reach a road. 30 yards to the left is a path going into Codmore Wood opposite.

Cross the stile, and follow this path half-left through thick woodland for about 200 yards, then bear right onto a wider track. In another 150 yards, branch left into another part of the woods, and in a further 200 yards or so, the path veers slightly to the left to reach a field. Cross this large field diagonally to your right, aiming to pass 50 yards to the left of a barn, to a metal gate, to reach a road at the entrance to Latimer. Turn right and walk along the road for half a mile, passing the Dog House, Parkfield, Latimer Mews, Latimer House and St Mary Magdalene Church.

> **Latimer House was built in 1832/38 for Lord Chesham, on the site of an earlier house. It became the National Defence College, and is now a conference centre.**
>
> **The church was rebuilt in 1867 by Sir George Gilbert Scott.**

A little way past the church, go through a gate on the left and cross a field, passing to the left of a clump of Scots pine and a wooden animal. A kissing gate on the other side of the field leads across a drive and down into the small and very attractive village centre.

> **The diminutive green, in addition to the village pump and war memorial, has a memorial to a horse. Lord Chesham fought in the**

Boer War and when a notable adversary, General Villebois, was killed, Lord Chesham gave his horse a home in Latimer, naming it Villebois in honour of its owner. On its death, its heart was buried here on the green, along with its ceremonial trappings.

Take the right-hand side of the triangle, and turn right again along the road, past School Cottage, for 100 yards. Turn left, following the Chess Valley Walk for the next three quarters of a mile, keeping on the path just above the flood plain, and passing on the way the tomb of two members of the Liberty family.

For a short way the path goes alongside the river, before reaching the farmyard of Mill Farm and passing the farm shop. This is Chenies Bottom. We leave the Chess Valley Walk here, and turn right, crossing the river and the millstream, and passing the old mill, to a triangle off the Chesham to Chenies Road. Take the right-hand side of the triangle, and cross the road with great care to enter another wood. Take the left fork and follow the path as it climbs up through the wood. At the top left-hand corner of the wood it becomes an enclosed path, and ahead you will see the distinctive chimneys of Chenies Manor. The path soon runs between brick walls, giving glimpses of the churchyard on the left and the renowned Manor gardens on the right. At the main entrance to the house turn left.

Chenies Manor House was for four hundred years the home of the Dukes of Bedford, and the present house dates from the 15th and 16th centuries. The chimneys are a particular feature and are similar to those at Hampton Court. Henry VIII and Elizabeth I stayed at the house a number of times. It is said that Kathryn Howard accompanied the king on one of his visits and committed adultery with Thomas Culpepper, one of the king's attendants, and the ghostly footsteps which are sometimes heard approaching the queen's bedroom are those of the king. The gardens were created by the present owners and have frequently appeared on television gardening programmes. *House and gardens are open from April to October on Wednesday and Thursday afternoons and on bank holidays.*

The parish church of St Michael contains the Bedford Chapel, originally built in 1556 and described by Nikolaus Pevsner as "the richest single storehouse of funeral monuments in any parish church in England". Unfortunately, we can only glimpse them through the glass partition which divides the chapel from the main church.

Walk down the broad gravel drive to the village green.

The parish was known as Isenhampstead until the 13th century, when it became known as Isenhampstead Chenies, after the Cheyne family who owned the manor before John Russell, the first Earl of Bedford, acquired it by marriage. The name eventually became shortened to Chenies. It is very much an estate village, with most of the cottages rebuilt in an attractive style in the 1840's and 50's. The appropriately named Bedford Arms pub is 200 yards down the Chorleywood Road opposite.

On reaching the green, bear round to the right, in front of the school. Keep right, passing the school playground, and when the road bears left, go straight ahead along a gravel track, with a nice view shortly of the manor and gardens across to the right. At a T-junction of tracks turn right, and on reaching farm buildings, turn left through a metal gate onto another track. Follow this track as it bends slightly to the right, and there is suddenly a wonderful view of the Chess Valley across to Latimer. Continue ahead, along this panoramic track, known as Lady Cheyne's Walk, as it enters a wood. When the track meets a road, turn right onto the road for 50 yards, taking great care, and then walk ahead along the public bridleway in the next wood. As you reach the edge of this wood, turn right and continue in the wood, with the edge on your left. Go past a sports field, a pavilion and a car park. You soon reach a crossing path where you turn left to leave the wood and emerge on a private road with houses on either side. The private road becomes Chenies Avenue. Walk the whole length of it, crossing Elizabeth Avenue, and turn left onto another road at the end. After 100 yards, turn right onto the private footpath into Chalfont and Latimer Station.

Little Chalfont grew up around what was originally Chalfont Road Station, opened in 1889. Before that it was just a few isolated farmhouses and cottages on the turnpike road from Hatfield to Reading. This was called the "gout road" because Lord Salisbury is said to have built it to travel more easily from Hatfield House to Bath, to take the waters.

WALK 4: AMERSHAM TO GREAT MISSENDEN

A pleasant and varied walk, taking in Amersham Old Town, with its wealth of ancient and attractive buildings, the upper Misbourne Valley, secluded Little Missenden and a sampling of the Chilterns plateau, before descending to the valley again at Great Missenden.

8 miles

Travel

Amersham and Great Missenden are served by a frequent train service on the Chiltern Line between Marylebone and Aylesbury. Amersham also has regular buses (except Sundays) from Watford, Slough and Beaconsfield, and (including Sundays) from High Wycombe and Chesham. There is a bus service between Great Missenden and High Wycombe, but not on Sundays.

Refreshments

There is a good choice of restaurants, cafés and pubs in Amersham-on-the-Hill and Old Amersham, Little Missenden has two pubs, and Great Missenden a number of pubs, cafés and restaurants.

Route

Amersham-on-the-Hill grew up around the station on the Metropolitan Railway, opened in 1892, and was very much part of "Metro-land". The last edition of the book of that name, published by the railway company in 1932, advertises the new Weller Estate of 78 acres adjoining the station as "beautifully situated 500 feet above sea level". Houses ready for occupation were for sale at £875 with £25 deposit.

From Amersham Station, turn left and left again under the bridges, cross the road by the traffic island, and walk down the hill for 200 yards until you see the sign "Parsonage Woods" on the right. Enter the wood, a typical Chiltern beech wood, and follow the footpath up to the left along the edge

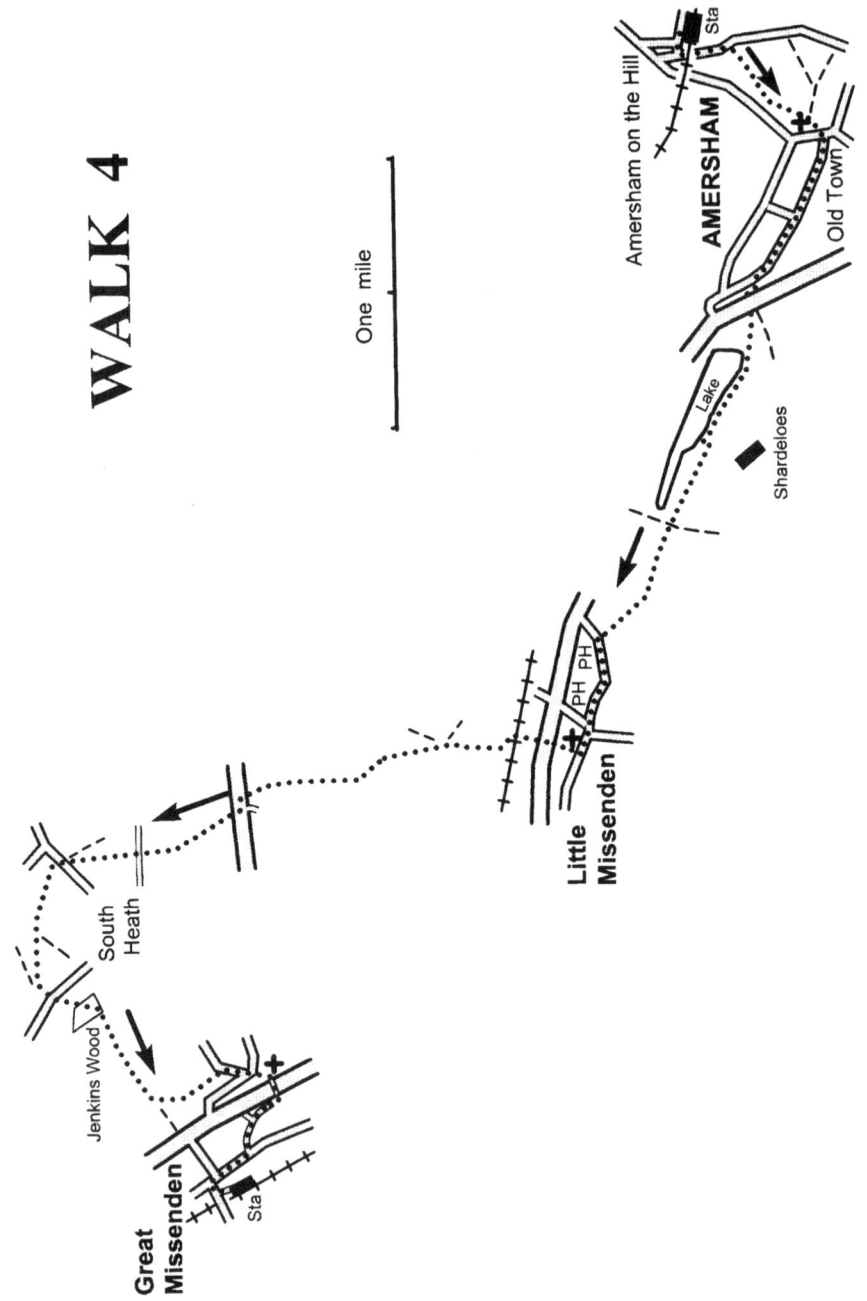

of the wood. Continue along this path, with glimpses through the trees down into Old Amersham. At a fork bear slightly left downhill, and continue just inside the wood, until you come to a tarmac path, where you turn left. Go down the path, fork left at the bottom and turn right over, then alongside, the River Misbourne towards the church.

Over the years the Misbourne used to dry up occasionally, and it was said locally that this always heralded disaster. In recent times it has only flowed irregularly, due to over-abstraction by the water companies and to climate change. At the time of writing, a multi-million pound scheme was in progress to increase flows once more. We hope that you are now walking beside a living river.

Bear left across the churchyard to the Broadway.

The exterior of the parish church is Victorian – the result of the restoration of 1890. The interior is light and airy. Its chief glory is in the monuments, most of which are in the Drake Chapel – not normally open to the public.

Turn right into the Broadway. We shall follow the Broadway and its continuation as the High Street for the next three quarters of a mile.

You are now in Amersham Old Town. Most of it is a Conservation Area, and no wonder! The buildings on either side of the High Street are from many periods, yet form an harmonious whole. The only jarring note is the inevitable large number of parked cars.

You will shortly come to the Market Hall, given to the town by Sir William Drake of Shardeloes (which we shall see later) in 1682. Note the parish pump of 1782, and behind it the old lock-up. The upper floor is still used for meetings, and market stalls are set up under the arches on Tuesdays, Fridays and Saturdays.

Amersham was an important post for stagecoaches and several of the inns had courtyards and stabling. Much more recently, two of them – the Crown (opposite the Market Hall) and the half-timbered King's Arms (a little further along), both featured in the film *Four Weddings and a Funeral*. In 100 yards, (also across the road) is Elmodesham House, the largest house in Amersham Old Town, and so called after the name given by Domesday Book to the town.

31

At no. 49 is the Amersham Museum, with a range of displays on the history and life of the town, and in particular local crafts and industries such as lace, chair and brick making. There is a copy of the original charter granted to the town by King John in 1201 for a fair, which is still held annually in the High Street. The building itself, part of a medieval hall house of c1450, is typical of many of the houses in the old town, with interiors much older than the facades. *Open from Easter to October on Saturdays, Sundays, and bank holiday Mondays, and on Wednesdays in the school summer holidays, 2.30 to 4.30 pm.*

Further along, no. 129 is the smallest house in Amersham. On the other side of the road are the Drake Almshouses, built in 1657 by the then squire to house six poor women of the parish. A little further, at the junction with Mill Lane, is the 17th century Town Mill. Nearly opposite is Little Shardeloes, dating back to Tudor times.

Just past the last house on the left is a road sign "The Chilterns" marking the boundary of the Chilterns Area of Outstanding Natural Beauty. 100 yards past this, the tarmac path bears off to the left, goes alongside the bypass for 100 yards or so, then dips under it and arrives at the gates to Shardeloes House. Go through the gates and follow the South Bucks Way sign to the right. Cross two cricket fields, passing just to the left of the pavilion, to a kissing gate beyond. If a match is in progress, you may feel it tactful and safer to follow the boundary and pass to the right of the pavilion. Go though the gate and straight ahead, still keeping on the South Bucks Way. On the right you will soon see Shardeloes Lake with its numerous wildfowl, although in recent summers it has sometimes dried up.

At the top of the hill opposite is Shardeloes House, built in 1758/66 for William Drake, replacing an earlier house which burnt down. The original architect was Stiff Leadbetter, but Richard Adam subsequently took over, and it is now considered his earliest complete country house. As you will have gathered, the Drakes were the squires of Amersham. A Francis Drake married into the family which owned the Amersham estate in 1637, and came to live at Shardeloes. The Drakes subsequently occupied the house until the present century. It is now divided into flats. The grounds were laid out by Humphrey Repton, but have gently declined into agricultural land.

Towards the end of the lake the path veers slightly to the left to two stiles. Cross these and continue straight ahead. At the end of the field cross a bridle path and go over a stile. Our route, and the South Bucks Way, follow the Misbourne for the next mile to Little Missenden, joining a track on the way, which then joins the road through the village. Go over the cross-roads in the village centre.

On the right is the manor house, built in the 16th and 17th centuries, and soon afterwards the charming village church. From the outside, an unusual feature is the dormer window. Inside, it is renowned for its medieval wall paintings. The most striking is one of St Christopher carrying the infant Christ across a river, in which fish may be seen swimming. The nave and chancel arch are Anglo-Saxon or early Norman, and there is a fine Norman font. To the right of the paintings is a replica of a medieval statue of St Catherine (the original was stolen), a touching memorial to Olivia Dahl, who died at the age of eight, the eldest daughter of Roald Dahl, the best selling children's author and his film actress wife, Patricia Neal. Olivia's grave is in the small cemetery beyond the village school. Roald Dahl lived at Gypsy House in Whitefield Lane, Great Missenden until his death in 1990.

Immediately after the church, take a footpath on the right, cross the course of the infant River Misbourne, cross the very busy A413 with extreme care, walk up the footpath opposite and cross the railway bridge. Turn left into the wood and climb steadily upwards until you come to a track leading from the farm on your right. Turn left here, follow the track downhill as it bears slightly to the right, leaves the wood and crosses an attractive dry valley, very much a feature of these chalk uplands. Follow the track up and round the edge of the wood, bearing right, left and right again, enjoying the fine views down into the Misbourne Valley. At the wood corner, the track turns left and crosses the field to another wood. Follow the edge of this round to the right and at the end, where the track turns left, climb a stile and carry on in more or less the same direction, diagonally across a field to a stile on the other side, aiming some way to the right of a large white house "The Hyde" which comes into view as you cross. Continue ahead along the edge of another small field with a fence on your left, and cross another stile onto an enclosed path. This leads into the drive of The Hyde, which in turn will take you to the B485.

Turn left, and in 50 yards, opposite Hyde Lane, cross the road carefully, and follow the Great Missenden Circular Walk (which you will do for most of the rest of this walk) straight across the field opposite, over a stile and across the next field keeping to the same line. Go straight ahead along the right-hand edge of the next field, cross a stile and walk between hedges, cross a road with traffic humps, continue along another enclosed path between gardens, eventually continuing in the same direction along an unmade road (Marriots Avenue) until you come to a road with white lines down the middle, at the end of South Heath.

Cross the road and the stile opposite, and cross the subdivided field, with its smallholding, diagonally to the stile in the far corner. Once over the stile, turn left diagonally across the corner of the field to two stiles. From here continue in the same direction (following the Great Missenden Circular Walk) cutting across the corner of this large field, making for a stile in the hedge about 25 yards to the right of an electricity pole which is in front of a small wood. Climb this stile, turn left and follow the field edge to the corner of the wood.

Cross a stile, take the path ahead through the wood, and cross the stile at the other end into a long field. Make for a metal gate at the far end. Go over the stile by the gate, cross the road and follow the "public footpath" and waymark signs to a stile at the other side of the field. Climb the stile and cross the wood.

This is Jenkins Wood, and the earthworks around the perimeter mark the site of a medieval homestead enclosure.

As you emerge, bear right, again following the waymark signs, and walk along the right-hand side of a wire fence. Cross a stile and go straight ahead and down the valley, keeping to the left of a small wood. At the bottom corner of the field you will find a stile. Once over this, immediately cross another stile to the left, and follow the right-hand path as it twists and turns near the bottom edge of the wood, with views of Great Missenden below. At the far corner of the wood the path continues alongside a small paddock, a riding area and a farmyard, then becomes a farm drive. Keep ahead along the drive to join a road. Follow the road for 100 yards to the B485 at Frith Hill. Cross over with care and go down some steps opposite. Pass through the kissing gate ahead and bear left onto a drive which passes a graveyard and then Great Missenden Parish Church.

The church of St Peter and St Paul dates from the 14th century, with later alterations and additions. The font is similar to that in Little Missenden; both belong to the "Aylesbury Group" of fonts, all thought to be the work of a group of masons working in the 12th century.

The drive becomes a road as it crosses the Great Missenden bypass by a bridge. Follow the road as it turns right, and descends to a pretty corner of Great Missenden village.

On the way down, Missenden Abbey can be glimpsed through the trees on the left. It was founded in 1133, and after its dissolution in 1538 was converted into a private house. It has changed much over the years, and now serves as both a management training centre and an adult education centre. *Neither the Abbey nor the grounds are open to the public.*

Keep left at the bottom of the slope, to walk along Church Street.

On the left shortly is the Abbey Farmhouse, based on the original gatehouse of the Abbey.

In a few hundred yards you will reach the High Street. The signpost opposite says "Amersham 4½", but tell yourself that you came the pretty way! To find the station turn right along the attractive High Street, take the first road on the left (Station Approach), then left again shortly.

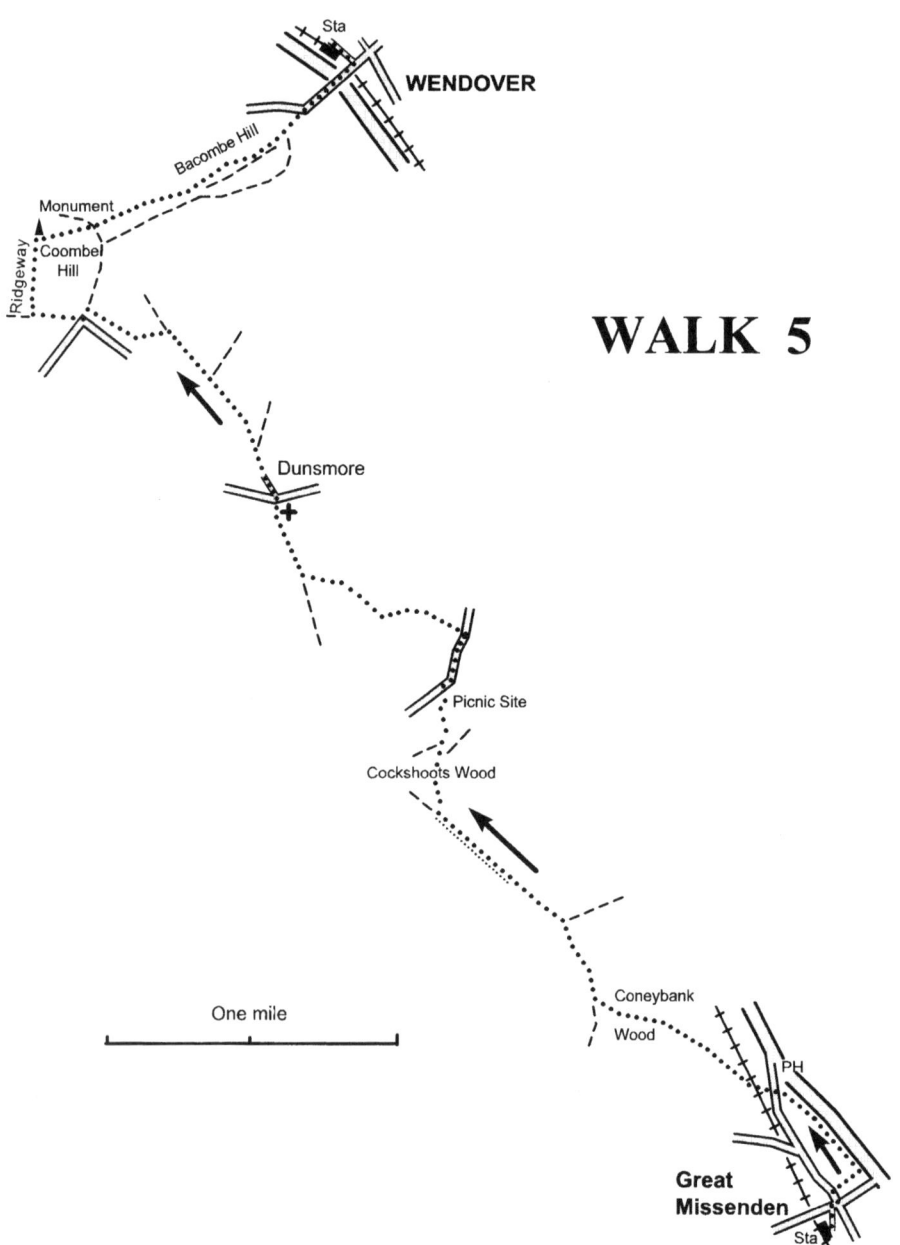

Sta

WENDOVER

Bacombe Hill

Monument

Ridgeway

Coombe
Hill

WALK 5

Dunsmore

Picnic Site

Cockshoots Wood

One mile

Coneybank
Wood

PH

**Great
Missenden**

Sta

WALK 5: GREAT MISSENDEN TO WENDOVER

An enjoyable and varied walk starting in the Misbourne Valley, through pasture and woodland, culminating on the Chiltern escarpment at Coombe Hill, with one of the finest views in the county, before descending to the charming small town of Wendover. The bridleways in the middle section can be muddy in wet weather. The energetic walker could combine this walk with Walk 6 to make a day long hike.

7 miles

Travel

Both Great Missenden and Wendover are on the Chiltern Line between Marylebone and Aylesbury via Amersham. Buses link Great Missenden with High Wycombe (but not on Sundays), and Wendover with Aylesbury.

Refreshments

There are pubs and restaurants at Great Missenden, and Wendover has several pubs, a tea-room and restaurants. Apart from the Black Horse three quarters of a mile from the start there are no pubs en route. Don't be deceived by a "PH" on the Ordnance Survey map at Dunsmore – there used to be two, but they are both now private houses. There is, however, a convenient picnic spot with tables at Cockshoots Wood, nearly half way. There is often an ice cream van in the car park approaching Coombe Hill.

Route

On emerging from Great Missenden station turn left, then right down Station Approach. At the High Street turn left, then right down Walnut Close. At the end take the tarmac path to the left of no. 18 and go ahead, with an electricity sub-station on the left and a car park on the right. After a stile bear left, where the route picks up the South Bucks Way, which is followed for the next two miles. Cross two further stiles next to gates, and continue ahead between a line of bushes on the left and the road hedge on the right. Where the bushes end, bear very slightly left and make for a stile at the end of the field, then head across the next field to the Black Horse public house, a popular centre for hot-air ballooning. Walk a few yards along the road to the right, then cross it with care and pick up a path, to the left of Town End Farm drive.

On the left is Mobwell Pond, fed by springs, and the source of the River Misbourne. In recent years it has often been dry.

The path leads to a railway underpass. Once through this, turn right, diverging from the railway to a stile in the hedge about 100 yards to the left of the railway line. Next bear slightly left uphill to another stile.

A notice just before the stile informs us that the field we are coming to is an Open Access Area. This is part of the Countryside Stewardship Scheme whereby landowners are given grants to enhance and conserve landscape areas, and access to the public is encouraged.

Go up steps and straight ahead towards the wood corner, then along the edge of the wood, following a wire fence on the left. At the end of the field cross the stile into Coneybank Wood, which in spring is carpeted by bluebells and other wild flowers. At a junction with a bridleway, at the end of the wood, turn right.

If you look through the hedge opposite at this point, you will have a good view of the dry valley known as Hampden Bottom, and in the far distance, amongst trees, can be seen Hampden House. Walk 7 goes past this, the family home of John Hampden.

Continue along this bridleway for another 500 yards, with fine views soon opening up across the upper Misbourne Valley to the right. At another junction bear left and follow inside the left hand edge of a small wood. On leaving the wood continue along the hedged bridleway. A footpath runs parallel on the other side of the left-hand hedge, and can be a useful alternative route if the bridleway is muddy. After a quarter of a mile the bridleway joins the drive of a house, where we continue straight ahead. In another 250 yards (where the parallel footpath comes out) we leave the South Bucks Way and take the bridleway on the right, at a tubular metal gate. Follow the blue arrows on trees and posts in a generally northern direction, ignoring all crossing paths until reaching Cockshoots Wood picnic site.

The picnic area was given to Buckinghamshire County Council by the Little Hampden Estate, and benches and tables have been provided.

Leave the car park and turn right into Cobblershill Lane, being mindful of the traffic on this narrow country lane. After 350 yards turn left over a stile to cross a woodchip horse-riding track, and then go ahead across a grass field to a gateway at the top corner of the field. Continue uphill following a rough track with the hedge on the right, and bear right through two more gateways, then follow a meandering right-hand hedge. Cross a stile by a metal gate to follow a hedged track until a junction is reached near "Hampdenleaf". Here turn right along a track to Dunsmore ignoring paths to the left and right.

Go ahead at a crossroads, taking the lane signposted "Dunsmore village only". Keep ahead on the bridleway when the made-up surface peters out. Ignore the first stile on the left, but keep left at a fork shortly afterwards, to pass over a stile next to a barrier, and continue in woodland between barbed wire fences. After half a mile, and about 200 yards beyond a crossing track with a cattle grid, look out for a footpath on the left (yellow waymark arrow). Take this and follow it downhill through the trees for 200 yards, ignoring a minor cross-path, to an open brackeny area at the bottom and another cross-junction of paths. Here turn right along the bottom of the valley and after 250 yards (having ignored a path to the left, and going straight ahead over another cross-junction) look for a yellow arrow on a tree on the right. Turn left almost immediately (another yellow arrow will confirm that you are on the right path), to eventually emerge at a car park near a road bend.

Head slightly left across the car park entrance to a pedestrian gate. Bear left, with a fence on the left and gorse scrub away to the right. In 300 yards the Ridgeway national trail comes out of the wood on the left, and we follow it as it bends round to the right and along the edge of the hill, with wonderful views opening up immediately.

The Countryside Commission's Ridgeway long distance path starts at Overton Hill, near Avebury. From there to the Thames at Goring it follows the prehistoric track along the Wiltshire and Berkshire downs. For the rest of its 85 miles, it takes a more convoluted route, sometimes on the Icknield Way, sometimes on the Chiltern escarpment (as now), but also through woodland and farmland. Several of the walks in this book follow the Ridgeway for stretches, and it's nice to meet the "serious" hikers and backpackers on it as well as those, like ourselves, out for a ramble.

You are now on Coombe Hill. This 106 acres of chalk downland was given to the National Trust in 1918 by Lord Lee of Fareham. Lord Lee also bequeathed his home, Chequers, to the nation to serve as the official country residence of the Prime Minister. If you look down and over to the left soon, you will see the house coming into view. A better view of it is obtained from Walk 7, which crosses the main drive.

The Chiltern Hills, of course, include not just the open downland of the escarpment, but mature beech woods, rough common, heathlands, dry valleys and the farmland of the plateau, where the chalk is overlaid by clay with flints. Half of the walks in this book are on the Chilterns, and demonstrate the variety of scenery.

Continue along the edge of the hill, gradually climbing, until you see a monument ahead. Make for this.

The monument was erected in 1904 as a memorial to the 148 Buckinghamshire men who died in the Boer War, and is 64 feet in height, constructed of Aberdeen granite. It has been struck by lightning twice, in 1938 (after which it had to be substantially rebuilt) and in 1974.

At 852 feet (260m) this is one of the highest points on the Chilterns. The panoramic view takes in the ridge in both directions, and also gives a superb bird's eye view of the Vale of Aylesbury. Just below the monument a topograph points out other landmarks, including two of the great houses built in Buckinghamshire by members of the Rothschild family. It doesn't mention the nearest, Halton House, which can be seen in the woods beyond Wendover.

At the monument turn right and follow the Ridgeway waymarks downhill, taking the slightly lower path initially. When you reach a sign for Bacombe Hill, go straight ahead as the Ridgeway makes a short diversion to the left.

Just before reaching the very bottom, note a signboard on the left, which gives some interesting background information about Bacombe Hill nature reserve and about the management of areas like this.

The path now arrives at a road. Cross this carefully and continue downhill. Turn left after the road and railway bridge for Wendover Station, or go straight ahead for Wendover itself.

Wendover will be described in more detail at the beginning of Walk 6. The centre of the town is very attractive, and makes a relaxing place to wander in now that the traffic is whisked past it on the new bypass.

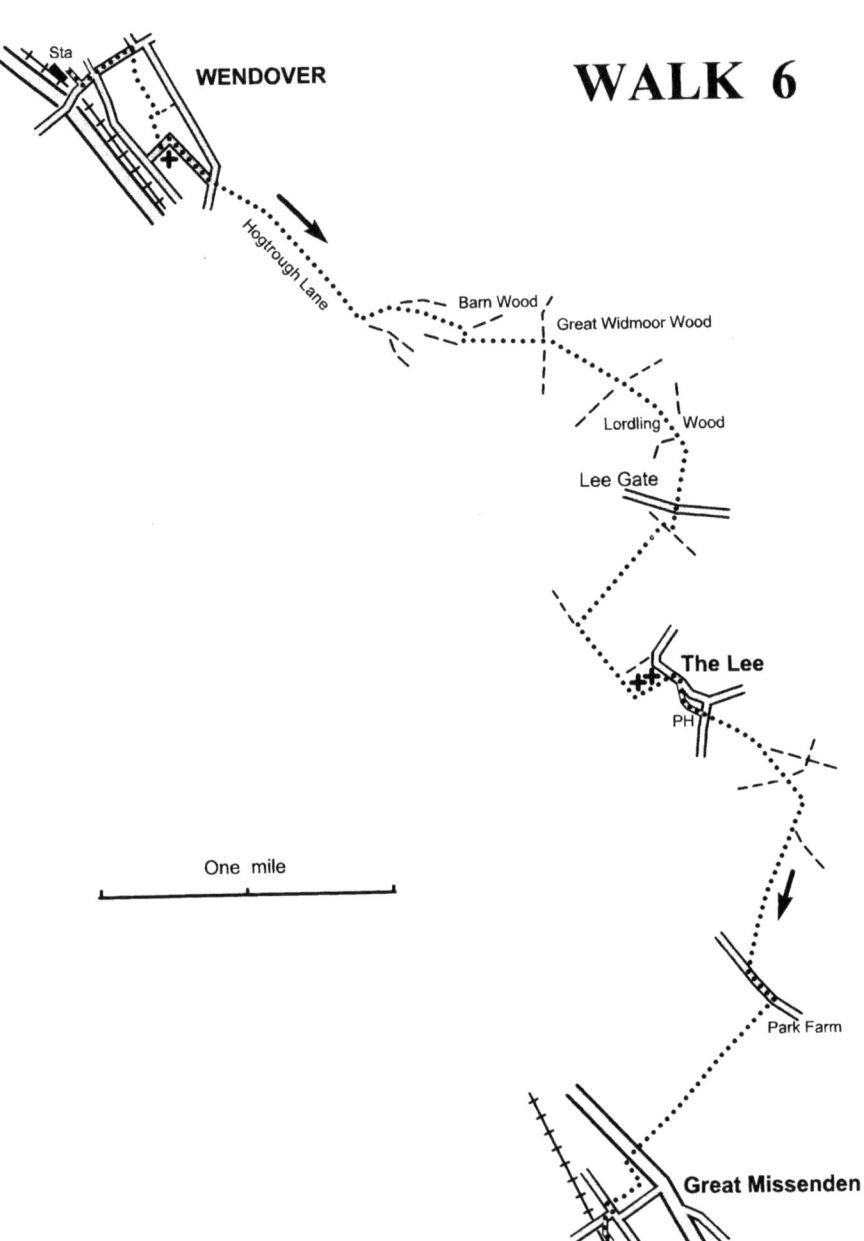

Sta
WENDOVER

WALK 6

Hogtrough Lane

Barn Wood

Great Widmoor Wood

Lordling Wood

Lee Gate

The Lee
PH

One mile

Park Farm

Great Missenden

Sta

42

WALK 6: WENDOVER TO GREAT MISSENDEN

A pleasant walk, following the Ridgeway national trail out of Wendover, then through woodland onto the Chiltern plateau, and eventually down into the Misbourne Valley. This walk could be combined with Walk 5 to make an all day walk of 14 miles.

7 miles

Travel

Wendover and Great Missenden are both on the Chiltern Line between Marylebone and Aylesbury via Amersham. Buses link Great Missenden with High Wycombe (but not on Sundays), and Wendover with Aylesbury.

Refreshments

Wendover has a number of pubs, a tea-shop and restaurants. There is one pub – the Cock and Rabbit at The Lee – on the walk, and there are pubs and restaurants at Great Missenden.

Route

From Wendover Station, turn right up Station Approach, then left to walk down Pound Street, which shortly becomes the High Street.

Wendover is strategically situated at the entrance to one of the gaps through the Chilterns. The High Street is on the Ridgeway national trail and also on the line of the Icknield Way, a trade route dating back to prehistoric times connecting Salisbury Plain and East Anglia, the main centres in the Neolithic period, and running below the ridge of the Chiltern Hills.

The open area on the left of the High Street is known as the Manor Waste, and is where the market is held every Thursday. A little further down on the right is the 17th century Red Lion. Oliver Cromwell is said to have stayed there in 1642. Robert Louis Stevenson visited in 1875 and admired the wood panelling in the parlour. Rupert Brooke was also a visitor. At the bottom of the

High Street is the distinctive red brick clock tower, built in 1842 by the then Lord of the Manor as a market hall and lock-up; the tower was added in 1870. The building now houses the tourist and community information office, and the parish council offices. A little way along the Tring Road ahead is a group of cottages supposedly given by Henry VIII to Anne Boleyn.

Just before the clock tower turn right to follow the Ridgeway path. Continue along the tarmac and concrete path (known as the Heron Path or Rope Walk) through Heron Park, beside the stream whose crystal clear Chiltern water still feeds into the long abandoned Wendover Canal. Ignore a metal footbridge and bear right, away from the stream, to pass the mill pond and emerge opposite the church gate.

St Mary's parish church is 14th century but was considerably restored in the 19th century. *Open Sunday afternoons.*

Turn left and follow the minor road for 400 yards to a crossroads. Cross over to make the gradual ascent of Hogtrough Lane.

300 yards after passing a large farm and cluster of buildings on the left, bear left to follow the Ridgeway path at a junction, and keep left at another fork almost immediately. At another junction in 100 yards fork right and climb gradually uphill. After 500 yards, near the top of the rise, bear right at a signpost, here leaving the Ridgeway, and at the top of the slope turn left onto a track. Follow this track, ignoring side branches, until reaching a crossing track. Here go straight on, ignoring paths to the left and right, and you should eventually pass a concrete Ordnance Survey triangulation pillar (shown on the map as 232 metres, or 761 feet). Continue for 300 yards, passing a field on your left, and at a main crossing track go ahead through Lordling Wood among tall, graceful beeches. On joining a track bear left past a house garage. In 100 yards, at a public footpath signpost, turn right to follow a right-hand hedge down to a road near Lee Gate.

Turn left for 20 yards, cross the road with care, then go right opposite "Whitecot" to follow another right-hand hedge. After crossing a stile, turn right for 20 yards, then left to follow a narrow path through trees. Ignore a crossing path, and by a gateway go ahead to cross a stile and follow a right-hand hedge. Keep to the right of a pond, and emerge to keep a hedge on your left. At the end of the field turn left to pick up the Chiltern Link path which is followed for most of the next three quarters of a mile. After passing by a belt of trees, a hedge appears on the right, and at a junction with a track go ahead over a stile heading just to the left of a house with a white gable end. Go over a gravel drive between two stiles, turn right over another stile, to follow a path beside two churches.

The first is the old parish church of The Lee, dating from the 13th century. It was originally a chapel of ease, served until the 16th century by the monks of Missenden Abbey. There are some interesting wall paintings, which were not discovered until 1965. At the top of the east window is some rare 13th century glass. Below are Art Nouveau style stained glass portraits of three notable puritans – Oliver Cromwell and two from Buckinghamshire: John Hampden (see Walk 7) and Miles Hobart, who was MP for Marlow and in 1626 was imprisoned for two years for locking the door of the House of Commons against the King's Messenger.

The new church, further on, was built in 1867/69. Just past it, over to the left, is a separate area containing graves and memorials to members of the Liberty family. The most striking is a tall Celtic cross in Art Nouveau style, a memorial to Arthur Lasenby Liberty, founder of Liberty's of Regent Street. He bought the manor and built or improved many of the houses in The Lee at the beginning of the century. The whole of the churchyard is a conservation area – part of the National Living Churches and Cemeteries Project for Conservation. *The keys to both churches may be obtained from the Vicarage, 200 yards along the road to the left.*

Turn right from the churchyard and fork right at the village green, to reach the Cock and Rabbit.

Opposite the pub is a cairn of "pudding-stone", a type of conglomerate caused by the action of ancient river flows.

Turn right at the pub.

A diversion down the road for some 300 yards leads to an enormous wooden statue, which looms over the hedge on the left. This is a ship's figurehead of Admiral Earl Howe, and comes from the Howe, later renamed as HMS Impregnable, the last wooden warship built for the Royal Navy. When it was broken up in the 1920s, a lot of its timbers went into the rebuilding of Liberty's store.

After turning right at the Cock and Rabbit, go immediately left by Hawthorn Farm, on a road which soon becomes a stony track. Stay with the track as it bears right, ignoring the signpost for the Chiltern Link, which we now leave. Go ahead at a track crossing, passing a cottage, then Field End Grange, on the right. Just after passing a memorial seat, turn right over a stile by a metal gate and follow a right-hand hedge for about 200 yards. As the hedge bears right, strike out slightly left across the field to a stile, and continue in the same direction over a succession of stiles to an arable field, where the path heads for a large oak tree to the left of a house, and emerges onto a road.

Turn left for 150 yards, then go right at a public footpath sign on the tarmac drive to Park Farm. 200 yards along the drive, just before a gateway, keep left and follow a narrow enclosed path between hedges. At an iron kissing gate keep ahead, following a left-hand hedge with views over Great Missenden in the valley below. Continue downhill in the same direction following a rutted track. Cross the very busy A413 with great care. (There is an underpass to the left, but it's not a right-of-way). Take a path opposite, turning left and climbing two stiles, before turning right over a stile by an electricity pole, leading onto an enclosed path. Keep ahead bearing right and left by a house (no. 20). A cul-de-sac (Walnut Close) leads up to the main road, where you turn left, then right and left again for Great Missenden Station.

WALK 7: LITTLE KIMBLE TO LACEY GREEN

A classic Chilterns walk, taking in some of the finest and most typical scenery, with an opportunity to see some remarkable wall paintings and cross the Prime Minister's front drive. There are interesting links with history and the walk ends by one of the oldest windmills in Britain.

9 miles

Travel

There is a good bus service between High Wycombe and Aylesbury stopping at Great Kimble and Lacey Green, although Sundays could be a problem. Some trains on the Chiltern Line between Marylebone, High Wycombe and Aylesbury call at Little Kimble station: very few on Mondays to Fridays, more on Saturdays, but none on Sundays.

Refreshments

There are pubs at Great Kimble, Little Hampden and Lacey Green, and another – the Pink and Lily – is a third of a mile off the route.

Route

Bus passengers should alight at the stop for Little Kimble church, a quarter of a mile north of Great Kimble. If arriving by train, turn right on leaving the station, cross the road and walk for about 300 yards until you reach the Wendover turning on the left. Before starting the walk proper it would be a shame not to visit the little parish church, on the right just a few yards down the Wendover road.

All Saints Church, Little Kimble, is renowned for its fine 14th century wall paintings, arguably the best in Buckinghamshire. The collection of saints includes St Francis preaching to the birds, St Christopher, St James and St George. In the chancel is a group of floor tiles from the 13th century, with an Arthurian theme.

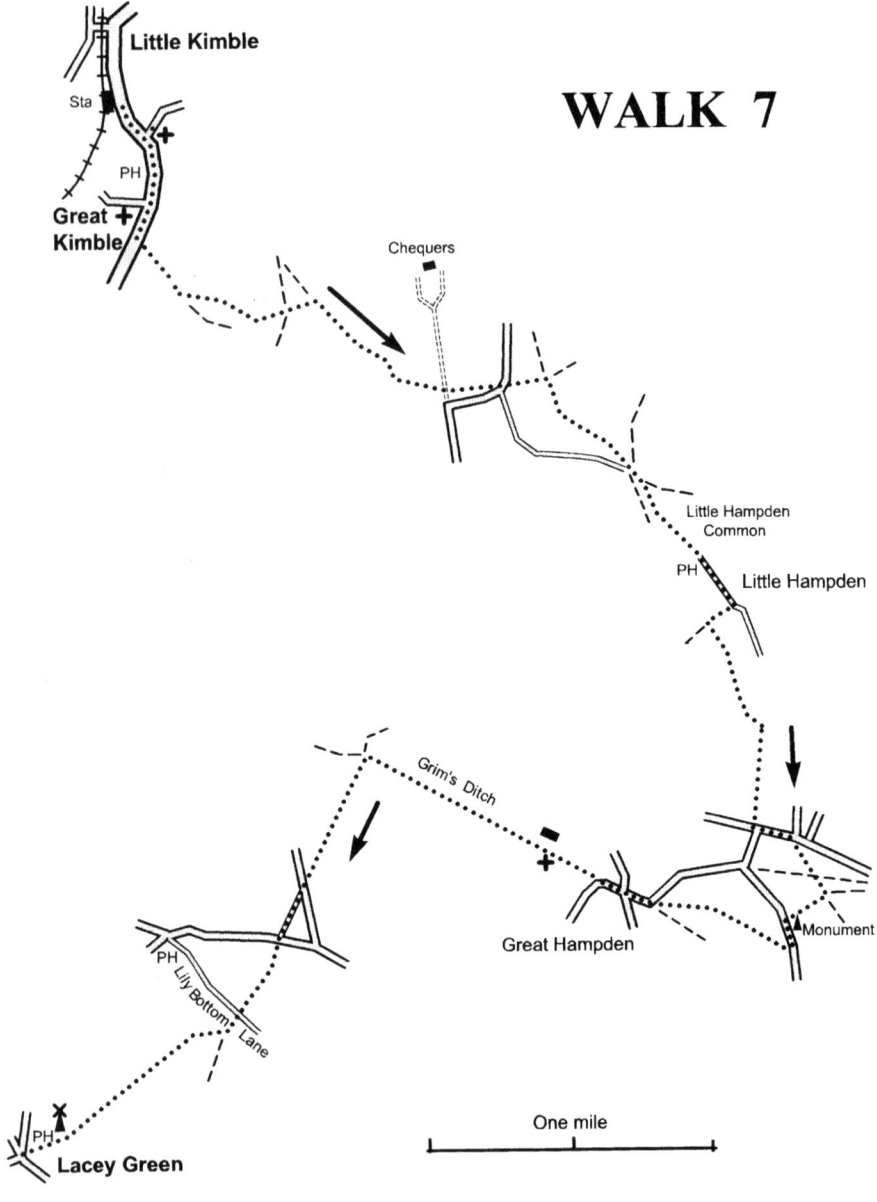

WALK 7

Little Kimble

Sta

PH

Great
Kimble

Chequers

Little Hampden
Common

PH   Little Hampden

Grim's Ditch

Great Hampden

Monument

PH   Lily Bottom Lane

PH
Lacey Green

One mile

On leaving the church turn left, left again at the main road, and at the end of the layby cross this very busy road with great care and continue on the footway over the brow of the hill, passing the Bernard Arms, to Great Kimble Church.

A board by the churchyard gate commemorates John Hampden, a local and national hero of his time. His refusal, at a meeting in this Church in 1635, to pay the ship money tax demanded by Charles I, was the first in a series of events which led to the Civil War. John Hampden (known as the Patriot) played a leading part in the war, raising a regiment of Buckinghamshire militia against the Royalists. He died on 24th June 1643 at Thame, after being mortally wounded at the Battle of Chalgrove Field in Oxfordshire. A copy of the list of those who, along with John Hampden, refused to pay the ship money is framed on a wall inside the church.

Recross the road, again extremely carefully, and in 100 yards turn left up a gravel track (signposted "North Bucks Way"). Follow the track for a quarter of a mile, as it climbs steadily, then bear left through a kissing gate (opposite a field gate on the right). The path slants upwards over rough grassland. After 150 yards take a fainter path on the left, which crosses a ditch, bears slightly right and contours the hillside, passing a large beech tree, to join the Ridgeway path at a signpost by a fence corner.

This area of rough grassland is a marvellous spot for wild flowers and butterflies in spring and early summer. At any time of year the views behind and to the left are superb.

Follow the Ridgeway path ahead, alongside a fence bordering the head of "Happy Valley", and climbing to a kissing gate. Beyond the gate go ahead on a cross-field path. Pass through a further gate at the other side of the field, turning slightly right (with woodland on the right and fields on the left). The large house, initially hidden by trees, which soon becomes visible to the left, is Chequers, the official country residence of the Prime Minister.

The house is essentially a Tudor manor house built (or possibly rebuilt) in 1565, and altered and enlarged at various times since. It passed through various hands over the years, eventually coming into the ownership of Sir Arthur Lee (later Lord Lee of Fareham). He presented it to the nation in 1917, with many conditions for its preservation. In moving the second reading of the Chequers Estate Bill in the House of Lords, Lord Curzon said: "Standing in one of

the most romantic sites in the Home Counties, amid typical English scenery... itself an example of the most characteristic period of English architecture... this is a unique possession for which the nation will be grateful and for which its future occupants will be more grateful still". One of the peers did suggest, though, that if a Prime Minister was doing his job properly he wouldn't have time for weekends in the country. Since then the house has played host to many world leaders attending conferences or on state visits.

As the view ahead widens to include the Chequers lodge gate, the path passes into the edge of the wood beside a gate and bends right. In a few yards, at the end of the wood, turn sharp left and head across the field, aiming to the left of the lodge. Cross the drive to Chequers (it's difficult to avoid a feeling of being under security surveillance at this point!), passing though three kissing gates, and continue over the next field to a ring of trees, then bearing right towards some houses. Carefully cross the road here, and take the track ahead (still following the Ridgeway signs); this follows a belt of trees up to the edge of woodland. At the edge of the wood, leave the Ridgeway (which continues straight ahead) and turn right onto the signposted South Bucks Way. Occasional blue arrows on tree trunks are a help on this next section. Follow the track gradually uphill (ignoring a path branching right after a few yards). At the top of the hill the path continues ahead as the track bears left. The path later rejoins the track, with a replanted area to the left, then forks left to emerge at the junction of several paths at the end of a road. Continue to follow the South Bucks Way, the right-hand of two paths leading approximately ahead, as it rounds a wooden barrier onto Little Hampden Common.

You may feel disconcerted that this doesn't look like a common. It was certainly more open in former years. In 1928 there was an outcry when the owners tried to enclose it because of "thoughtless abuse of the privilege of access". It seems members of the public were driving cars across the common and lighting fires.

Continue across the common, first through bracken and then woodland, and straight ahead on joining a bridleway from the right, to emerge at the end of a road by the Rising Sun. Walk along the road for about a quarter of a mile to a small triangular green with a seat. Turn right here, leaving the South Bucks Way, onto a tarmac/gravel track. This ends at Warren Cottage (where a grassy track continues ahead). Turn left here onto a field edge path (with a hedge screening a farmyard on the left). Follow various bends in the hedgerow as it gradually descends into the valley.

The view to the left as you descend is of an attractive and typical Chilterns dry valley These were probably formed in the Ice Age when rivers were more abundant and the chalk subsoil was frozen and impermeable.

At the field corner the path continues in the same general direction but with the hedge now on the right, making for the right hand end of a coniferous plantation in the valley. After passing the plantation, the path emerges at a road junction. Turn left, (towards Great Missenden), using, for safety, the broad verge on the right-hand side of the road. Opposite the side road to Little Hampden, turn right into the corner of a wood and follow the path diagonally across the wood. A stile leads onto a grassy vista with views of Hampden House to the right and the curious "pepper box" lodges to the left.

The vista is known as the Queen's View and is said to have been created by John Hampden's grandfather to improve the view from the house for Queen Elizabeth I when she stayed there. The pepper boxes were added later; each consisted until recently of one room, one box containing the kitchen/living room, the other the bedroom.

At the far side of the open space a further stile leads into the corner of the next wood. Follow the path ahead along the edge of the wood. On reaching the next corner, turn right at cross paths, still close to the edge of the wood and climbing gradually. Ignore a path to the left just before an old pit, and cross a stile out of the wood at the wood corner. Cross the field ahead to emerge on a road just to the right of a monument.

The monument was erected in 1863 in honour of John Hampden and his refusal to pay the ship money levied "without authority of the law".

Turn left along the road, passing Honor End Farm on the right. After the end of the buildings (now converted into houses) take a path on the right. Continue ahead for 100 yards, then bear half right to a stile. Bear half left along the field edge. Follow this field edge path towards the wood ahead, with a hedge and views of the valley to the right. On entering the wood, the path bears slightly left; continue across the wood to emerge onto the corner of a road, over a stile beside a gate. Follow the road ahead and over a crossroads. Just past the crossroads you will see a grass-covered bank on the right. This marks Grim's Ditch, which we will follow for the next two miles.

It is thought that these extensive linear earthworks date from the Iron Age, and were probably built to mark territorial boundaries, rather than for military purposes.

Where the road turns left, keep straight on along the drive of Hampden House to reach Great Hampden Church and a converted stable block on the left, and Hampden House on the right.

The church contains an impressive monument to John Hampden and a memorial to his wife with a poem he wrote himself. *The church is only open for services, or by appointment.*

The Hampdens owned the estate from before the Conquest to the present century. Most of the house dates from the first half of the 18th century and it is one of the earliest examples of the Gothic revival. The stable block is from the same period. *Not open to the public.*

Walk straight ahead, through two gates, and follow the field edge on the right, ignoring the diagonal cross-field path on the left. A few yards after a gate on the right, there is a choice between a field edge bridleway and a path along the band of trees on the right, reached through a gap in the fence. The latter is recommended, as it follows a well preserved section of Grim's Ditch. Where the field boundary turns sharp left, the paths continue ahead, with the footpath crossing to the other side of the bridleway. After about a quarter of a mile, turn left at cross-paths. (Grim's Ditch does the same). The path soon leaves the wood and follows the field edge on the right. At the far corner of the field, the wood is re-entered by a stile, and the path continues, to emerge at a road junction, for the last 150 yards actually going along the top of the bank by Grim's Ditch. At the junction follow the road ahead (signposted Lacey Green) to the next junction, then continue straight ahead on a bridleway, which passes through more woods to emerge (after being joined by two paths from the left) at a house. Pass the house to a lane.

A detour for a third of a mile up the lane (Lily Bottom Lane) to the right will take you to the Pink and Lily public house. It is named

from Mr Pink, the butler at Hampden House and Miss Lillie, a parlourmaid, who set up home together, and established the pub, around 1800. It was a haunt of Rupert Brooke, who used to call in at the pub on his walks in the Chilterns. A not very good verse he dashed off on one of his visits is framed on the wall.

Turn left and then, after a few yards, right along the side of a building. An enclosed, often muddy, track leads uphill. After about 100 yards, as the slope eases, cross a stile on the right. Walk diagonally left across a field to a stile in the hedge. Make for the far right-hand corner of the next field, keeping to the right of a pylon. Continue ahead over a stile, now with a fence on the left. After four more stiles, bear slightly right across a dip to a stile in a hedge beside a tree and in line with the windmill. Cross the next field to a hedge corner, then continue with a hedge on the right. After three more stiles, with the windmill to the right, emerge onto the road at Lacey Green.

The windmill is the oldest surviving smock mill (that is, where only the cap turns into the wind, rather than the entire mill) in the country, reputedly dating to 1650. It originally came from Chesham, but was moved to its present site in 1821. After being derelict for many years it was restored to working order by volunteers from the Chiltern Society. *Open Sunday and bank holiday afternoons, May to September.*

The Windmill access road and the Whip public house are immediately to the right. The bus shelter on the left is for the service to High Wycombe. The stop across the road is for buses to Princes Risborough, Little Kimble and Aylesbury.

WALK 8

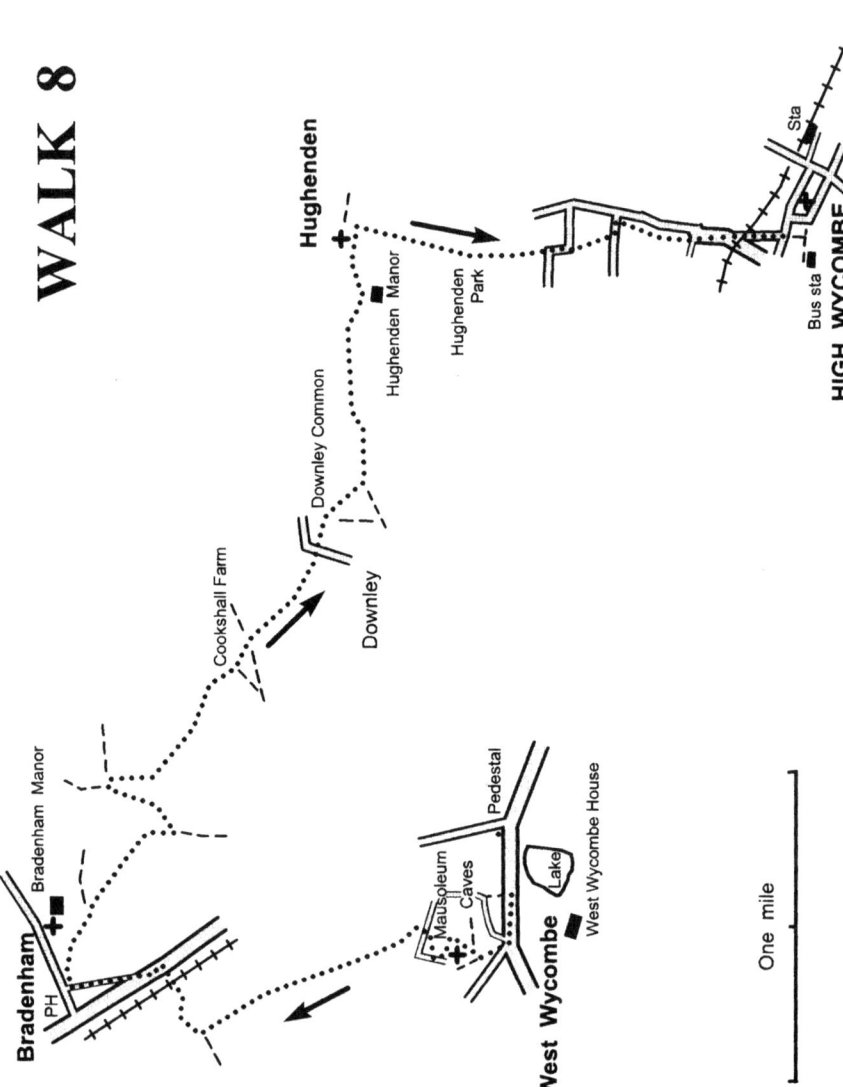

Hughenden

Downley Common

Cookshall Farm

Bradenham

Bradenham Manor

PH

Downley

Hughenden Manor

Hughenden Park

Hughenden Park

Sta

Bus sta

HIGH WYCOMBE

West Wycombe

Mausoleum

Caves

Pedestal

Lake

West Wycombe House

One mile

54

WALK 8: WEST WYCOMBE TO HIGH WYCOMBE

A pleasant and varied Chilterns walk visiting three unspoilt, and very different, National Trust villages.

7 miles

Travel

West Wycombe is well served by buses from High Wycombe, with services also from Oxford, Thame, Princes Risborough and Aylesbury. High Wycombe is on the Chiltern Line, with frequent trains from Marylebone to Aylesbury or Banbury and the Midlands, and is at the hub of a network of bus services.

Refreshments

There are pubs and cafes at West Wycombe (including a cafe at the caves and another at the garden centre near the start of the walk), a pub at Bradenham, and the tea shop at Hughenden Manor is open when the house is open. Not surprisingly, there are many pubs, cafes and restaurants in High Wycombe. Walkers wishing to avoid the last, increasingly urban, mile and a half, can pick up a bus at the main road at the bottom of Hughenden's drive (but not on Sundays).

Route

Most buses from High Wycombe stop at the Swan public house, although some stop only at the Pedestal and do not enter the village. For passengers from Stokenchurch or Oxford, the stop is towards the eastern end of the village.

West Wycombe village was acquired by the National Trust in 1934, and has been carefully preserved since then, with no jarring note to mar the effect of the mostly 16th to 18th century houses, built from local materials. At 21 High Street is the oldest building, the 15th century Church Loft, originally a rest house for pilgrims. At the eastern end of the village is an unusual milepost – the Pedestal – erected by Sir Francis Dashwood in 1752. It gives the miles (in Roman numerals), but travellers are left to work out for

themselves out which is "The City", "The County Town" and "The University".

Walk, in the direction away from High Wycombe, to the junction with the road to Bledlow Ridge, at the west end of the village, opposite the gates to West Wycombe Park.

West Wycombe House and park are largely the creation of the second Sir Francis Dashwood and are now in the care of the National Trust. The graceful house (completed in 1771) sits naturally in the landscaped grounds. The best view of the grounds, as was clearly the intention, is from the house itself, where the various features, including the lake, the Temple of Venus, the Temple of Music, several bridges, and even the church on the summit of the nearby hill, all blend harmoniously in an apparently natural landscape. *House and grounds are open June, July and August on Sunday to Thursday in the afternoon; the grounds only are also open in April and May on Sunday, Wednesday and bank holiday afternoons.*

Take the Bledlow Ridge road (Chorley Road) from the junction. A few yards after West Wycombe Hill Road on the right, take the sunken path bearing right, then turn up steps nearly opposite the car park entrance. A marker stone indicates routes, to the church or the caves. Take the left-hand, uphill route unless visiting the caves.

West Wycombe caves are the result of large amounts of chalk excavated from the hillside by Sir Francis Dashwood, in order to build the straight main road which leads to High Wycombe. This created work for some 40 local unemployed farm workers. Sir Francis was a founder member, along with other pillars of the establishment, of what became known as the Hellfire Club, which met for bacchanalian orgies at Medmenham Abbey, on the Thames between Marlow and Henley. Meetings of the club were subsequently held in these caves, when the original venue began to attract too much publicity. Sound effects, tableaux and a commentary provide the atmosphere for the modern visitor. *Caves and cafe are open 11.30 to 5.30; Monday to Friday, March to October; Saturdays, Sundays and Bank Holidays, all year.* If you have made a diversion to the caves, rejoin the original route by going up steps to the right when facing the entrance, then following a grassy path up to the mausoleum.

If not visiting the caves, our path slants uphill, with pleasant views opening up on the right, including, eventually, West Wycombe House, reaching steps up the steepest part. At the top of the steps turn left and head for the Dashwood mausoleum. Pause for breath, and the fine view of High Wycombe.

> The mausoleum (according to Nikolaus Pevsner, possibly the largest in Europe since classical times) was built by Sir Francis, paid for by a bequest from another member of the Hellfire Club. The urns in the alcoves were intended to hold the heart of each club member after death, but they never did. It does, however include a monument to Francis Dashwood's first wife, and, on one of the walls, monuments to the two wives of the first Baronet.

Walk to the right of the mausoleum, and take the concrete path through the churchyard and alongside the church.

> Although medieval in origin, the interior of the church was beautifully remodelled in the Palladian style. The nave is said to be based on the Temple of the Sun at Palmyra. Note the magnificent painted ceiling and the unusual font, resting on a slim column around which is entwined a snake. At the same time, the tower was increased in height and the golden ball added. The ball is a landmark for miles around and is said to seat ten people. John Wilkes, another member of the Hellfire Club, said that it was "the best Globe Tavern I was ever in." It is possible to climb the tower to just below the ball, to be rewarded with a panoramic view of West Wycombe village and park and over typical Chiltern scenery. *The church is open every afternoon in June, July and August; the tower on weekend afternoons from April to September.*

At the church door turn right to exit through the churchyard gate.

> As you leave the churchyard, note the perimeter bank. This is the boundary of an Iron Age hill fort, which would have dominated the valley below.

Now turn right to cross the car park, and go downhill straight ahead, making for the middle of a line of posts. As you approach them, a green post with a footpath sign becomes just visible by the road coming from your left. Cross the road to the sign, and follow it into woodland, with the hillside falling to the right. The path emerges from the wood along the top edge of a field, with views of the Bradenham Valley below, then re-enters woodland. It continues to follow the hillside, through pleasantly varied woods, for about three quarters of a mile. In places the route may seem a bit uncertain, but at any junction keep as level as you can, until you come to a T-junction with a wider path. Turn right, downhill, soon emerging from the woods, with a view of Bradenham ahead.

The railway below was the last main line built in Britain. The Great Western and Great Central Joint Railway was fully opened in 1910, enabling the Great Western to compete with its old rival the London and North Western Railway for the lucrative Birmingham traffic. Even at the end of the 1950's there were some ten steam-hauled expresses a day between Paddington and destinations such as Wolverhampton, Birkenhead, Chester and North Wales. In recent years the line has had a revival with a fast and frequent service of turbo diesel trains between Marylebone and Birmingham.

When the path reaches a farm, follow the farm road left under a railway bridge to the main High Wycombe to Princes Risborough Road. Cross this busy road with care and turn left along the footway. After about 150 yards (and soon after a private driveway) take a tarmac pedestrian way which soon becomes a minor road. Follow this until it reaches Bradenham village green and turn right onto a bridleway-signposted track up the near side of the green. (A detour to the Red Lion is just 150 yards down from the green to the left).

Virtually the whole of this pretty village, together with the surrounding estate, is owned by the National Trust. The manor house at the top of the green was rebuilt in the 17th century. Queen Elizabeth I was entertained there in 1566 on a journey from Oxford to Hampden House (see Walk 7). The owner at the time was Lord Windsor! In 1829 the manor came into the hands of Isaac D'Israeli. Isaac was the father of statesman and novelist, Benjamin Disraeli, who lived here at the family home, making several unsuccessful attempts to become Member of Parliament for Wycombe. His last novel *Endymion* describes "Hurstley" as his hero's childhood home and says of the woods behind: "It had once been a beech forest, and though the timber had been greatly cleared, the green land was still occasionally dotted, sometimes with groups, and sometimes with single trees, where the juniper which here abounded... gave a rich wildness to the scene". In 1838 he fell in love with Mary Anne, the wealthy widow of his friend

Wyndham Lewis; they married the following year and moved to her house in London. *Bradenham Manor is not open to the public.*

The parish church of St Botolph, across to the left, has a Norman south door and some interesting memorials. Isaac D'Israeli is buried here.

A National Trust noticeboard by the car park at the top of the green tells something of the history and natural history of the village, and the management of the estate.

Follow the track past the car park and continue uphill, with the wall of the manor grounds on the left, until the track enters woods. Turn right here, immediately before the track forks, onto a smaller path which initially climbs into the woods and then contours the hillside, some white arrows on trees offering some guidance, until the path joins a broader one. After a dip with a cross-path at the bottom, and a further climb with a path joining from the right and then one from the left, there is a break in the trees on your left with a power line in it. Turn left, not along the broad track, but to follow a path to the right of the power lines and a hedge, with a coniferous plantation on your right. When the path veers away from fields on the left, turn right at the next junction and right again at a stile in a dip.

Follow a small valley down to a gate, then turn left, alongside a fence. Follow this into the next valley and up the far side of it. A track continues ahead for about a quarter of a mile to emerge from the woodland at Cookshall Farm. Continue straight ahead, with the buildings on the left, to pass through a gateway into the next wood. Bear left, then slightly right and downhill, and cross another path in a valley bottom. Climb the opposite slope. At the top of the hill, leave the wood and continue with a hedge on the left, and views back towards West Wycombe on the right. After passing through two kissing gates emerge onto a road at Downley Common.

Cross the road and then continue ahead across the common, between the cricket ground and football pitch, making for the houses visible in the dip ahead. On leaving the playing field, the path bears slightly right, to leave the houses on your left, then more steeply downhill into woods. When you reach a junction of several paths at the bottom of the hill, turn left down the valley. At the edge of the woods continue along a fenced track between fields. At least in winter, Hughenden Manor becomes visible on the wooded ridge ahead. The track climbs the hill through woods to the manor gate. Turn half-left along the manor drive, passing the entrance to the house and gardens on the right and the National Trust cafe and shop in a stable block on the left.

Hughenden Manor was bought by Benjamin Disraeli in 1847, shortly after he became Member of Parliament for Buckinghamshire, and the year before his father died at Bradenham. He made major changes to the house and gardens, and lived there happily with his wife Mary Anne, as his political career flourished, becoming Chancellor of the Exchequer and then (twice) Prime Minister. He was made Earl of Beaconsfield in 1876, and in the following year entertained Queen Victoria at Hughenden. The house and the estate were acquired by the National Trust in 1947.

The interior of the house is much as it was in Disraeli's time, and many of the original contents remain. The formal garden, a terrace with attractive views around, has been recreated to reflect Mary Anne Disraeli's original design. *Open in the afternoon; March: Saturday and Sunday; April to October: Wednesday to Sunday and Bank Holiday Mondays.*

Continue to a cattle grid. Bear slightly right here, through a gate downhill to Hughenden churchyard, which you enter through a further gate, to the left of a row of cottages.

The church is mainly Victorian. On the chancel wall is a very personal memorial to Disraeli from Queen Victoria, said to be the only example of a memorial in a parish church erected by a reigning sovereign to one of her subjects. The pulpit is impressive, of marble and alabaster, with carved angels. There are also some attractive Victorian wall and ceiling paintings in the chancel, and a good number of stained glass windows, many featuring angels. The Disraeli tomb is outside the church, against the east wall.

We have described Hughenden as a National Trust village. In fact, there has never really been a village of Hughenden, except for this core of church, manor and a few other buildings. It is a scattered parish of former hamlets, now almost outlying suburbs of High Wycombe.

From the car park below the churchyard, turn right and head across parkland, making for a five bar gate just to the right of a sports ground and a line of trees marking the course of the river at the bottom of the valley. As you approach the gate you will see a stile just to the right of it. Cross the stile and carry on down the valley, veering slightly to the right. Just beyond a small lake (which may be dry) cross another stile. Keep on the path, through what is now Hughenden Park, managed by Wycombe District

Council, but was at one time part of the grounds of Hughenden Manor. Stay on the slightly higher ground as the river bears away to the left. Bear left to follow an avenue of mostly young trees.

The hill-top monument, visible from here over your right shoulder, was erected by Mary Anne Disraeli in memory of her father-in-law Isaac.

Make for a road just to the left of a factory building. Cross the road, carefully, walk along the right hand pavement, and when the road bears to the left, follow a footpath straight ahead. The next section of the path is alongside a wire fence next to factory buildings – a reminder that High Wycombe is essentially an industrial town.

When you reach a road turn left, and in about 100 yards cross over and take a footpath on the right. This goes alongside the river, now rather urbanised, but with surprisingly clear water and with a good variety of plant life. The path crosses the river and continues a further 100 yards to another road. Turn left here for 50 yards, passing the roundabout on your right, and cross the main road by a traffic island. Walk along the road to the right, keeping on the left-hand pavement, making for the furthest left of four viaduct arches. Once through the arch, the pavement widens and leads in a short distance to the centre of High Wycombe, with the bus and railway stations well signposted.

High Wycombe has been an important manufacturing centre and market town for centuries. In medieval times it had an important clothmaking industry, with mills along the River Wye; lacemaking was a cottage industry here as elsewhere in Buckinghamshire; papermaking was a major industry from the 16th century until very recently. Perhaps High Wycombe's greatest claim to fame, however, is as a centre for furniture making, which started in the 18th century with small-scale chairmaking, using the Chiltern beech woods, and developed into factory production by companies which became household names. The Wycombe Museum specialises in the history of chairmaking in the town. *Castle Hill House, Priory Avenue. Open Monday to Saturday (except bank holidays).*

Although there has been much modern development in the town centre, the High Street still has some handsome buildings. The Guildhall of 1757, Little Market House (from about 1604, remodelled by Robert Adam in 1761) and the nearby parish church make a fine group at the western end. The graceful church of All Saints is the largest in Buckinghamshire.

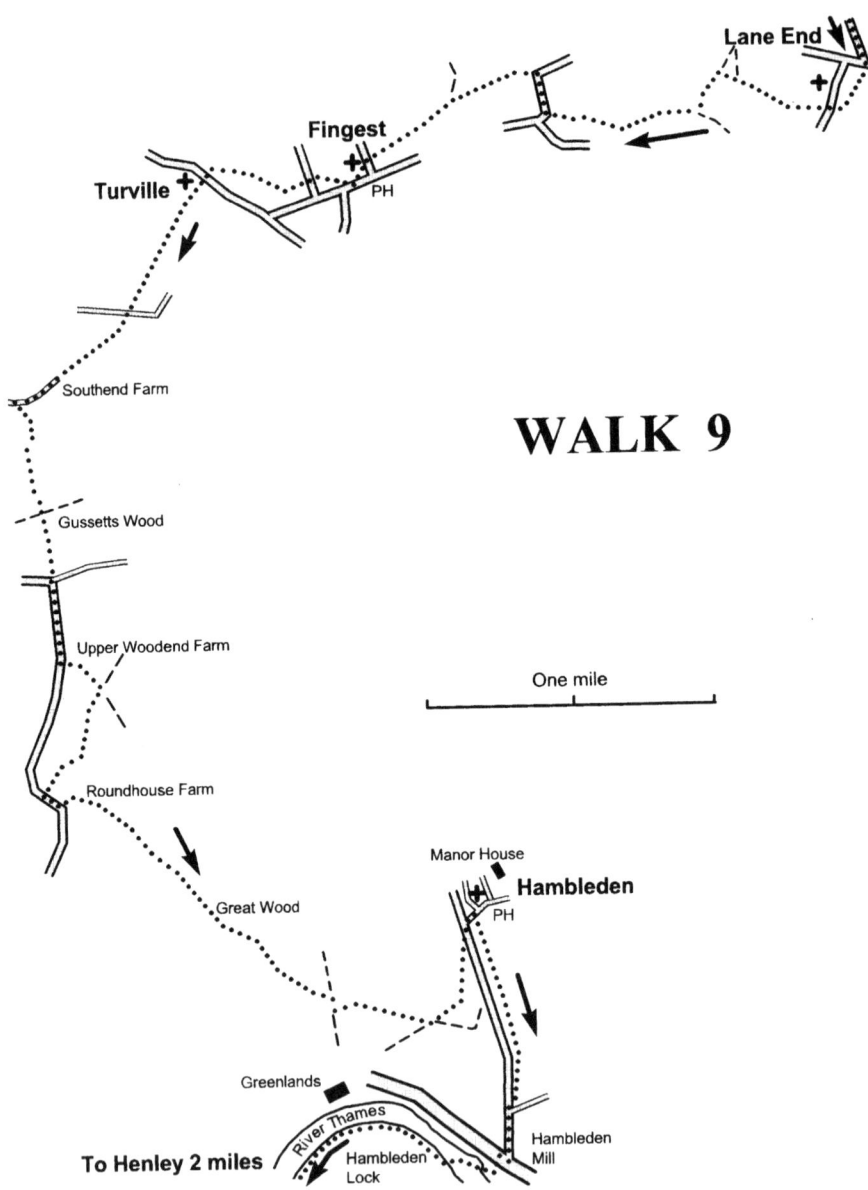

Lane End

Fingest

Turville

PH

WALK 9

Southend Farm

Gussetts Wood

Upper Woodend Farm

One mile

Roundhouse Farm

Manor House

Great Wood

Hambleden

PH

Greenlands

River Thames

To Henley 2 miles

Hambleden
Lock

Hambleden
Mill

WALK 9: LANE END TO HAMBLEDEN MILL

A walk through some of the best of the Southern Chilterns scenery, visiting three picturesque villages, and down the Hambleden Valley to the Thames, with an optional three mile riverside extension to Henley.

10 (or 13) miles

Travel

Lane End has a frequent weekday bus service from High Wycombe, though less frequent on Sundays. Hambleden and Henley are served by buses on the Reading, Marlow and High Wycombe route, but not on Sundays. There is also a bus service between Henley and Oxford. Trains run from Henley to Twyford, with connections to Paddington.

Refreshments

There are pubs at Lane End, Fingest, Turville and Hambleden, and one just off the route at Fawley. Henley has a wide choice of pubs, restaurants and tea shops.

Route

Leave the bus at Lane End village pond (actually one of two in the centre of the village). Walk up the road about 100 yards to the other pond. Here cross the main road and go down a narrow path just to the left of the Osborne Arms.

While this part of the village retains its charm, most of Lane End is now a dormitory suburb. In the 19th century Lane End was one of the centres in this area for chairmaking, linked with the local craft of "bodging" or chair-turning, which was carried out by local men working directly in the woods, using pole lathes.

On reaching a drive, cross and take the path ahead. Follow this as it goes by a wall, across the front of a house, then by a wall again for a further 100 yards. Where the fence on the right ends, bear right and go between trees to reach a road. Cross this and go down the drive opposite, which leads past the Forge Works to the former Jolly Blacksmith pub just beyond. Take a path on the right immediately after this building.

Go through a kissing gate and continue into the corner of a wood. The path descends to cross a bridge in a gully and then climbs again, keeping close to the edge of the wood. In about 300 yards, immediately after the wood-edge and the main path turn left, bear right to go downhill into another gully. When the path is joined by a bridleway from the left, continue ahead along the bridleway for about 20 yards before taking a path forking left, which reaches a stile at a corner of the wood. Cross the stile.

Take the field-edge path, with the wood on the right. Bear right after the next stile, still along a field edge, but re-entering the wood at the next corner. The path crosses the wood and leaves it over a stile. Go approximately straight ahead to follow the field edge, turning right at the next corner, to reach a stile at the far corner. Cross this and continue gradually downhill, with a fence on the left and bushes on the right. After the next stile the gradient steepens and the view widens to reveal Fingest down the valley.

From here on, there is a very good chance of seeing red kites. They were introduced some years ago on John Paul Getty's nearby Wormsley Estate and have bred very successfully. These magnificent birds of prey soar in wide circles for hours, and close to can be recognised by their deeply forked tails.

The path ends at a road; turn right along it for 300 yards, then go down a few steps to a stile on the left where the road bends right. Follow the hedge round to the left (avoiding another path which crosses the field to the right). After the next stile the path goes slightly uphill to the corner of a wood, with the hedge on your left. Pass a farm track down to a farm on the left, and continue ahead with the wood on the right. Another track joins from the right after about 200 yards. Beyond the far corner of the wood, where the track turns left, continue ahead over a stile onto a field-edge path, with Fingest church ahead. After two fields separated by a stile, pass between garden fences to arrive at a road, then go left for about 50 yards to reach the churchyard gate.

The most interesting feature of the church, apart from its lovely setting, is the large Norman tower with its later double saddleback roof. It been suggested that the tower originally served as the nave and that the present nave was then the chancel.

The path crosses the churchyard diagonally to another gate. A few yards to the right, the next path crosses a stile at the far side of a small green. Follow this, with a wall and fence on the left and a garden and field on the right, to the corner of a wood, where take the leftmost of three paths to emerge at, and cross, a road. The path contours the hillside before crossing a stile into a field. Descend across the field half-left to a small garden gate about 50 yards before the field corner, then follow the edge of the field to a kissing gate in the corner. Turn left immediately over a stile and down a stony track to the village green.

Turville is surely the prettiest village in the Chilterns, with its typical brick and flint cottages, small green, quaint half-timbered pub, village church in its quiet churchyard, all in a deep Chiltern Valley overlooked by a windmill. It's not surprising that it is often used as a setting for film and television. The windmill, for example, featured in the film *Chitty Chitty Bang Bang*. Author and playwright John Mortimer lives nearby, and the television film about his father, *Voyage round my Father* which was Lord Olivier's last role, was made here, as were the two television serials *Paradise Postponed and Paradise Regained*. More recently, the TV comedy series *The Vicar of Dibley* were filmed in Turville.

The parish church has a beautiful small stained glass window by John Piper, who designed the glass for Coventry Cathedral. He lived at nearby Fawley Bottom, just a mile from our route.

Cross the green towards the churchyard gate and turn up a narrow lane past attractive cottages. At the end of the lane continue ahead on an enclosed bridleway. This emerges into a field. Carry on straight ahead, ignoring paths to left and right, with marvellous views opening up of the upper Hambleden Valley. On reaching a gate to the left of a farm, cross the lane and continue in the same direction on a rough fenced track. The track bears to the right on reaching a wood. This is a good place to enjoy the classic Chilterns view behind, including the windmill above Turville.

Follow the track, up the hill through the small wood, and in 200 yards cross a stile by a gate, and continue in exactly the same direction along the crest of the hill through a field. Soon you will see the buildings of Southend Farm ahead. As you reach the farm, cross a stile beside the gate, and go ahead along the farm drive, keeping the farm buildings to the left. In 350 yards look for a stile on the left opposite a short post and rail fence and a five bar gate at the corner of a garden.

Cross the stile and the field beyond to the corner of the wood to the left of buildings in a dip. Enter the wood via a stile and descend a slope between holly bushes. Climb the opposite slope, keeping near the edge of the wood, to emerge into a field. Cross the field, aiming to the left of electricity poles on the skyline, near a group of trees. On reaching a fence, turn left to go alongside it (do not cross the stiles ahead). At the field corner, cross a stile and continue downhill in a wood. Cross a track in a valley and climb the opposite slope, bearing slightly left along the edge of conifers. At the top of the wood, cross a stile and the field beyond to a gate near the far left-hand corner.

Cross the stile by the gate and take the road ahead, signposted Fawley. In a quarter of a mile, at Upper Woodend Farm, take the concrete track which bears off to the left. Just before the concrete track ends, bear right onto a bridleway between hedges. In 200 yards cross a stile half hidden in the hedge on the right (almost opposite one on the left). Cross the field ahead, then follow the curving track to the left, with the fence on your right. Take a stile to the right, to pass to the left of converted farm buildings. Go through the gate to the drive ahead. Follow the drive to meet a road, and turn left along this for 150 yards. (The Walnut Tree public house is a further 300 yards along the road). Turn left along a track.

The tower was added to the farmhouse here in order to improve the view from Fawley Court, three miles away.

The track narrows to a path at a house on the left. There are pleasant views of the Thames Valley towards Henley. After fields on the right the path follows a ridge for almost a mile through pleasantly varied woodland, with occasional glimpses of the view beyond, eventually emerging from the woods to give fine views of the Thames between Marlow and Henley. Bear left downhill to cottages, and turn right onto the roadway past them.

You will see that the second cottage has a monogram "WHS" above the door. This is the first indication of WH Smith's association with Hambleden. Having made his money by building up a successful chain of newsagents from railway station bookstalls, he acquired Greenlands, the nearby house on the Thames and the large estate which went with it, including most of Hambleden. He went on to a successful political career, becoming eventually First Lord of the Treasury and Leader of the House of Commons, and was created the first Viscount Hambleden. On his death in 1895, he was buried in Hambleden churchyard.

After about 100 yards turn left onto a bridleway passing between hedges to reach the corner of a wood. Continue, keeping close to the lower edge of the wood. Ignore the first track branching left, but then turn left about 250 yards further on, opposite a path entering the wood through a gate from a field. The path to the left climbs through a clearing to a path junction. Continue straight ahead here, descending gradually. The final section, past the former school (given to the village by WH Smith), is tarmac. On emerging at a road junction, take the side road ahead towards Hambleden Village. After about 100 yards, our route turns right at a kissing gate just before a bridge, but it's worth continuing ahead to look at this very attractive village.

Hambleden has been described as one of the prettiest villages in England, both for the harmony of its brick and flint cottages, and for its position in the lovely valley running down to the River Thames. It has been in the ownership of the National Trust since 1944.

The parish church has several interesting features. There is a touching monument to Sir Cope D'Oyley, his wife and all ten of their children. Apparently, those who carry skulls died before their parents. In front of the memorial is an oak chest which belonged to Lord Cardigan, who led the ill-fated Charge of the Light Brigade. Some richly carved wooden panels used as an altar in the south transept are said by tradition to be from Cardinal Wolsey's bedhead!

As well as that of WH Smith, the churchyard contains the grave of Major George Howson, who started the tradition of wearing poppies on Armistice Day, and set up the factory for making them. There are also two 18th century mausoleums.

Beyond the church is the Manor House, originally built in 1603, and birthplace of Lord Cardigan. Also at the top of the village, and easily missed, is the Stag and Huntsman. As you leave Hambleden, note the graceful 18th century former rectory on the hillside just outside the village.

From the kissing gate, the path bends gradually right, keeping approximately parallel to the right-hand field boundary, to reach a kissing gate to the right of a small bridge. Cross a track here, and continue forward through the next field, again roughly parallel to the right-hand field boundary, and make for the right-hand corner of the field at the far end. Pass through a kissing gate at a road junction. Cross the side road, and continue on the pavement, initially on the left of the road, but crossing shortly before the junction with the main road. The bus stop for Henley and Reading is opposite the end of the pavement; that for Marlow and High Wycombe is a few yards to the left, beyond the road junction

Even if you are finishing the walk here, it is worthwhile continuing to Hambleden Lock. Turn right for a few yards along the main road, cross this busy road with extreme care, and go left down the far side of a cottage just beyond the gate to Hambleden Marina. On reaching a further gate ahead, turn right between wooden fences to reach the long walkway across the top of the weirs to the lock.

Hambleden Mill and the Mill House, to your right as you cross, together form one of the most photographed spots on the Thames. Both are 18th century, but there is said to have been a mill here since the 16th century.

Extension to Henley-on-Thames

If you are continuing to Henley, cross the lower lock gates and turn right. Directions are hardly necessary – simply follow the river bank for the next three miles. *There are, however, liable to be diversions during Henley Regatta week.*

We are now in Berkshire, and shall be until we cross the river again on reaching Henley. The large white house on the opposite bank in half a mile, is Greenlands, built about 1810 and later enlarged for WH Smith. It is now the Henley Management College. Though still a beautiful house, the effect is somewhat marred by the various modern extensions and annexes.

Another half a mile brings us to Temple Island, and at the further end of it is the elegant folly designed by James Wyatt in 1771. , We are now on the longest straight stretch in the whole course of the Thames. Just beyond the island is the start of the Henley Regatta course. In 1829 the first Oxford and Cambridge boat race was held here. The regatta has been held every year since 1839 and for a few weeks every summer the fields on this side of the river are full of tents and enclosures, and the river even busier than usual with boats of every kind.

In another quarter of a mile the handsome brick facade of Fawley Court can be glimpsed between the trees on the other side of the river. It is claimed that Sir Christopher Wren had a hand in the design of the house, which was completed in 1684. In the 1770's

James Wyatt carried out a lot of work to the interior, and around the same time the park was laid out by Capability Brown. Since 1953 the house has been owned by the Polish Congregation of Marian Fathers. *Open to the public from March to November, on Sunday, Wednesday and Thursday afternoons.*

On our side of the river is the small village of Remenham with its Victorian church. From here to Henley the path passes some interesting houses and rowing club headquarters. Approaching Henley, note the Edwardian boat houses on the other side.

As we near Henley Bridge, the path leaves the river for a very short distance. On reaching a road turn right to cross the bridge.

The elegant five-arched bridge replaced an earlier wooden one in 1786. The stone masks on either side represent Isis and Father Thames. Beyond is the impressive parish church, whose tower dominates the town, and has been visible since we rounded the bend in the river at Temple Island.

To reach the station, turn left once over the bridge. For buses, go straight ahead along Hart Street. Those for Oxford stop on the left before the traffic lights; those for Reading and High Wycombe stop on the same side beyond the lights, near the impressive Town Hall.

WALK 10

One mile

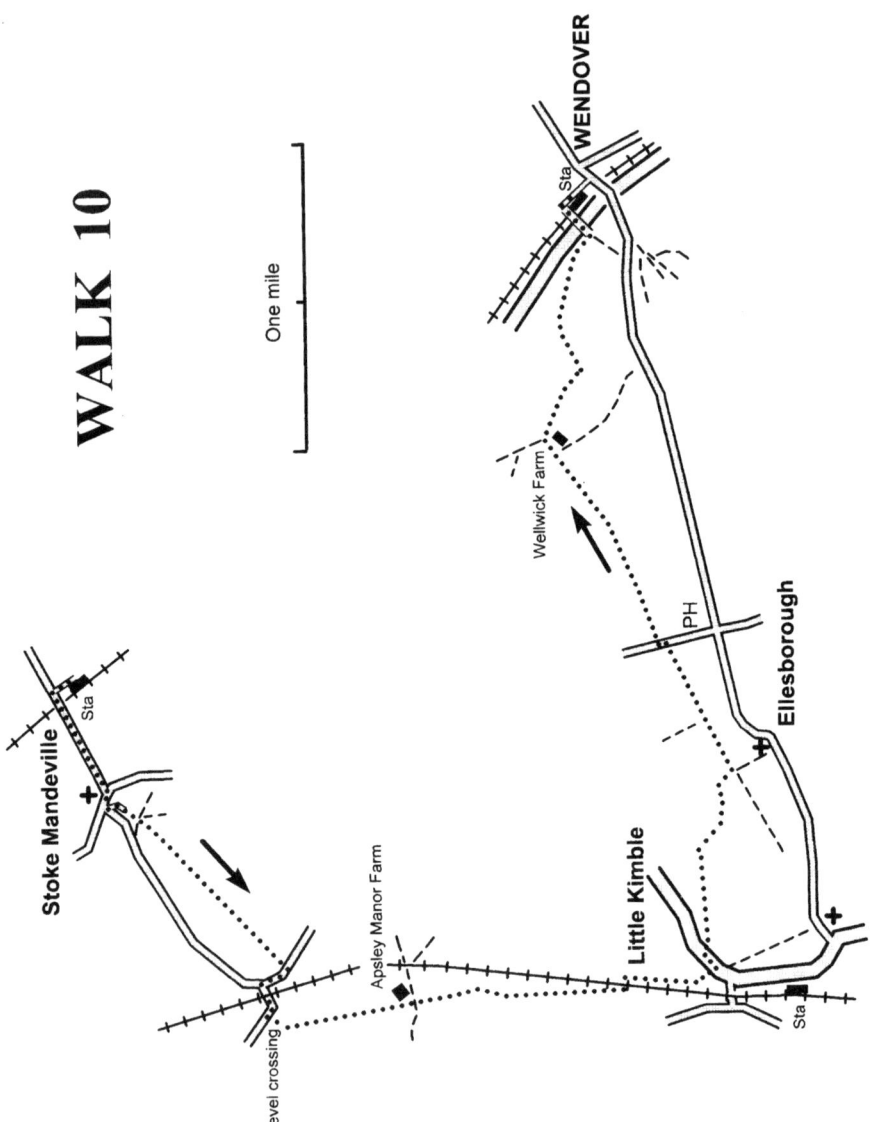

Stoke Mandeville
Sta

Level crossing

Apsley Manor Farm

Little Kimble

Sta

Ellesborough

PH

Wellwick Farm

Sta

WENDOVER

WALK 10: STOKE MANDEVILLE TO WENDOVER

The first half of this walk takes you through lush farmland on the edge of the Vale of Aylesbury, at times quite tough going, to Little Kimble. The second half is on higher ground with fine views of the Chiltern escarpment. The walk can be muddy in winter.

6 miles

Travel

Stoke Mandeville and Wendover are both on the Chiltern Line between Marylebone and Aylesbury. Both are served by a good bus service to Aylesbury, and buses also run between Stoke Mandeville and High Wycombe.

Refreshments

There are pubs at Stoke Mandeville and Wendover, and one at Butlers Cross, 300 yards off the route. The former Crown public house at Little Kimble is now the Kimble Diner, open all day. In addition Wendover has a tea-room and a number of restaurants.

Route

Until modern times, Stoke Mandeville was a very small village, where – it was said – "there's more crows than people". When the railway came to the village in 1892 it was suggested that "in the event of the dwelling houses being destroyed by fire or flood, the whole of the inhabitants can find temporary shelter in the station buildings".

On emerging from Stoke Mandeville station, turn left up to Station Road, noting the nice sculptures of two lions and a railway worker. Turn left again and walk along Station Road for about 600 yards.

The parish church was erected in 1866, replacing the original Norman church which was demolished. Most of the fittings, including a fine 16th century monument to four children of

Edmund Brudenell, Lord of the Manor at the time of Elizabeth I, were moved to the new church. The church was the setting of a cause célèbre in 1871. Two local boys claimed to have seen, through the window of the vestry, the young wife of the vicar committing adultery with a theological student. The vicar sued his wife for divorce. Not only was the case thrown out, but the two lads were tried at the Old Bailey for perjury and sentenced to two years and eighteen months hard labour respectively, much to the outrage of villagers. *Not generally open.*

At the roundabout bear right into Lower Road, cross the road carefully, cross the small green by a footpath, and then turn sharp left into Chestnut Way. Almost immediately a public footpath signpost on the left indicates the Stoke Mandeville circular walk which is followed for the next mile. Follow Chestnut Way as it bears to the right, and at the end take the footpath ahead between two bungalows. On emerging at a stile go straight ahead across a grass field to a footbridge. Continue ahead across two more grass fields with a stile between them. After crossing another stile, turn left for 10 yards into the next field, then right, following a field edge with a substantial elm hedge on your right.

At the field corner, cross a double stile and go straight across the field ahead to pick up another right-hand hedge. On emerging at a road turn right, go over a level crossing, and after 100 yards turn left onto a bridleway. Keep to the left of the buildings and just after the last one, cross the ditch on the left by a plank bridge and stile.

Our route now generally heads south for the next 1½ miles. Go half right across the field, heading for a gateway by the second tall tree from the left, then in the same direction to a pair of stiles and a plank bridge. Go half right across a field corner to a wooden footbridge. Keep ahead to converge with a right-hand hedge. Look for an iron gate on wheels on your right. Go through this and over a concrete bridge, turn left and follow a field edge with a stream on the left. In the next field continue alongside the stream, passing Apsley Manor Farm on your left.

The Manor of Appesley was first mentioned about 1215 in the Missenden Abbey charters, and the site still has a moat. The present building dates from the 16th century. A short detour over the bridge and along the track at this point will give you a view of the farmhouse and a glimpse of what's left of the moat.

After another quarter of a mile look out for a footbridge on your left. Cross this, turn right and continue in the same direction, this time with the stream on the right. Go over a double stile and continue ahead, gradually leaving the stream and converging with the railway line, which comes in on the left-hand side of the field.

This is the line from Princes Risborough to Aylesbury. It was opened as a branch of the Great Western Railway in 1863, nearly twenty years before Aylesbury got its direct line from Marylebone.

At the far left hand corner of this long narrow field, cross a white painted stile and go up the railway embankment steps. **Look out for trains before crossing.** Cross diagonally to the right, drop down, climb the stile and turn right along the field edge. After crossing a footbridge bear left away from the railway to the left of some mobile homes, to emerge onto the road at Little Kimble. To the right is the Kimble Diner restaurant.

Our route continues to the left, picking up part of the Ellesborough/Kimble circular walk. After 150 yards, cross over this busy road with care to a public footpath sign and stile. Go half-left across the field to a stile, cross a drive, pass a curious barn on your right and continue ahead, over stiles, through a number of fields with the hedge on the left for nearly half a mile.

Halfway along the third field, to the left of our path, are the mill ponds of a former corn mill, fringed by large native black poplar trees. The ponds are fed by a line of springs where the water from the Chilterns emerges.

After some power lines, about 70 yards after you cross a stile into a very large field, there is a gate on the left, by a large ash tree. Turn left here, and cross a stile into a small field.

There are now closer views of Coombe Hill with its monument in memory of the Buckinghamshire men who died in the Boer War. To its right and in the foreground stands Ellesborough Church. As the Parish Church for Chequers it is associated with a long line of British prime ministers. Further right is the conical shape of Beacon Hill, part of the Chequers Estate.

Cross another stile into a short enclosed path, then turn right and head to the right of a nearby large white thatched house. Cross the stile and turn left onto the tarmac track to pass Springs Cottage. Our route has now left the Ellesborough/Kimble circular walk and has picked up the distinctively waymarked Aylesbury Ring path which it will follow for the last two miles into Wendover.

Where the tarmac track turns right, take the enclosed path ahead to a grassy track across an arable field, then between the fences of horse paddocks, to reach a road near Butlers Cross. *(A diversion 300 yards to the right leads to the Russell Arms public house.)* Here turn left for 50 yards, and cross over to a public footpath sign and stile. Continue ahead, with the fence on the left, then on the right. The path then goes ahead across two arable fields and further stiles to Wellwick Farm.

The house dates from 1616, although the front is early Georgian. The rear retains the 17th century E-plan, and the tall octagonal chimney shafts are impressive.

Keep the buildings to your right, and bear right via two waymarked telegraph poles, then cross a stile onto a track between barns and houses. After leaving the buildings, turn left on a field track just beyond a fenced road for 50 yards, then right on a grass bank across the middle of a field (indicated by another waymarked telegraph pole). Where a hedge starts, turn left over a stile and follow a fence to another stile. From here go half right diagonally across a large arable field, heading towards the second pylon from the right. At a hedge corner continue with the hedge on your left. Near the cricket pavilion, turn left through a kissing gate, and along the right hand side of the cricket ground to a footbridge over the bypass and railway at Wendover station. To reach Wendover town, turn right then left at the top of Station Approach.

WALK 11: AYLESBURY TO WENDOVER

A canal-side walk, following the Aylesbury Arm of the Grand Union Canal through pleasant open countryside, then a short stretch of the main canal near its summit, finally along the largely disused Wendover Arm, now a haven for wildlife. This is longer than most of our walks, but the walking is easier, as it's mostly on level canal towpaths. There is a shorter alternative walk ending at Aston Clinton, or the walk can be ended at Marsworth.

15 (or 6/7) miles

Travel

Aylesbury is easily accessible by Chiltern Line trains from Marylebone via High Wycombe or Amersham, and has regular bus services from Oxford, High Wycombe, Milton Keynes, Luton, Watford, Tring, Hemel Hempstead and Leighton Buzzard. Wendover is on the Chiltern Line between Amersham and Aylesbury, with a good bus service to Aylesbury. Buses connect Aston Clinton with Aylesbury, Tring, Luton and Watford, and Marsworth with all except Watford.

Refreshments

Aylesbury has a full range of shops (including a superstore next to the railway station and another by the canal), pubs and cafés. There are two pubs and a canal-side tearoom at Marsworth, and Wendover has several pubs, a tea-room and restaurants. The PH shown on maps at Buckland Wharf is no longer a pub.

Route

If you intend to do the whole walk, you won't have much time to explore Aylesbury. However, it would be a shame if all you ever saw of the County Town were the railway and bus stations. Beyond the bus station is the Market Square (*antique market on Tuesday, general market on Wednesday, Friday and Saturday*). At the top of the Market Square is the National Trust owned King's Head Centre (*refreshments available*). It dates from before 1450, and was originally a monastery guest house. Beyond that is the

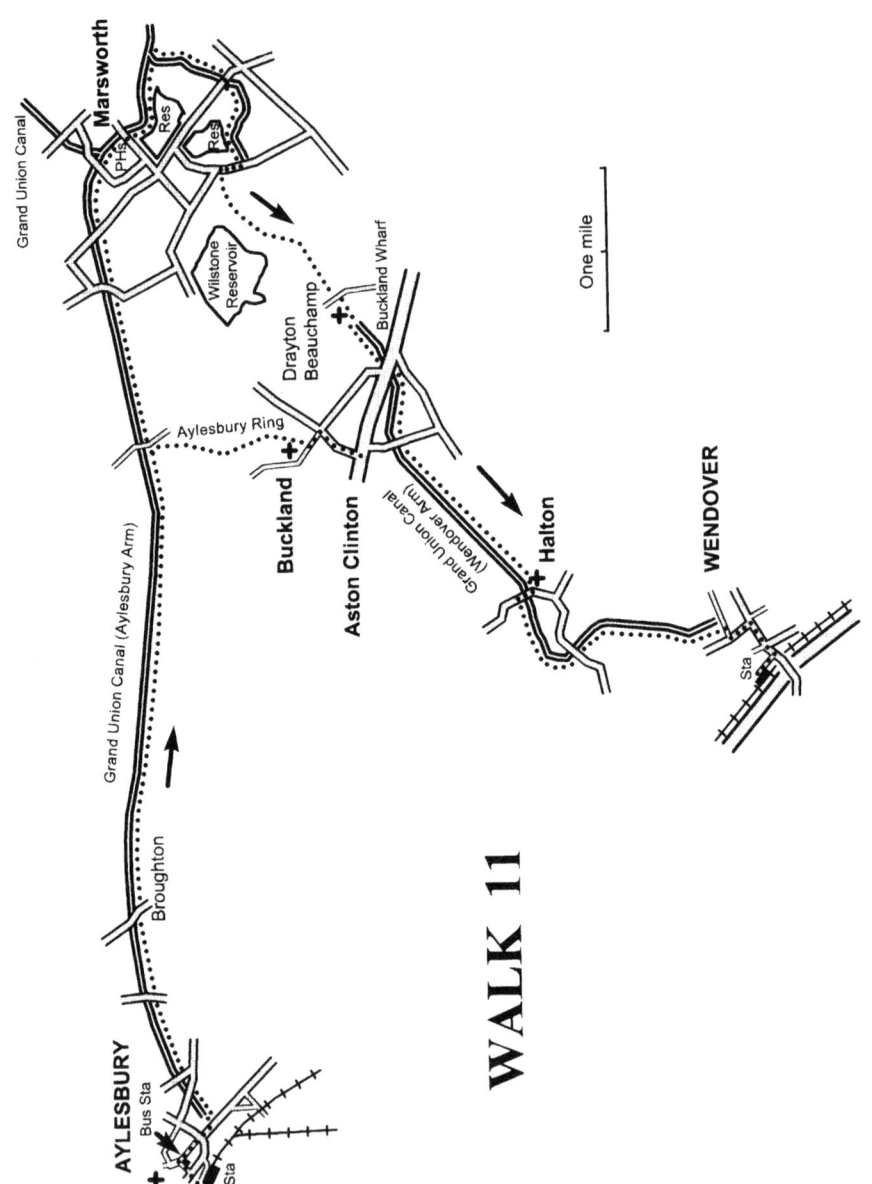

unspoilt Conservation Area leading to, and surrounding, St Mary's Square and the large and handsome parish church.

In Church Street is the splendid County Museum, recently refurbished, with displays on the history, environment, crafts and industries of Buckinghamshire, plus the Roald Dahl Children's Gallery and the Buckinghamshire Art Gallery. *Open Monday to Saturday 10 to 5, Sunday and bank holidays 2 to 5.*

From Aylesbury station follow the signs for the bus station: just past it turn right to walk down the left-hand side of Walton Street. Cross the roundabout at the bottom by a zebra crossing to the left and continue along Walton Street – now a dual carriageway. Just past the Ship Inn turn left and you will immediately see the canal basin in front of you, with the towpath to the right. Suddenly, you will find yourself in a different world. From here on, walking instructions are largely superfluous for the next six miles, as once the towpath is joined at the basin, it's simply a question of following it all the way to Marsworth!

A branch canal to Aylesbury was first mooted in 1794, although the scheme was not finally agreed until 1811. It opened in 1814 and was initially very busy, with substantial trade in both directions. However, fierce competition arrived with the Cheddington to Aylesbury branch railway in 1839. More sustained railway competition had arrived by the turn of the century with the coming of the Great Central and Metropolitan Railways. The canal's decline was thus speeded up, and by the Second World War trade on the arm had become spasmodic. Commercial traffic lasted until the 1950's, but the last regular delivery of coal to Aylesbury was in 1964. Since then, however, the canal's fortunes have been revived and sustained (after much effort by the Aylesbury Canal Society and other amenity bodies) by pleasure boating and other recreational interests. British Waterways, working with local and country authorities has carried out many improvements to the waterway and its infrastructure, ensuring its continuing attraction as a pleasant and inviting route, not least as a green "back door" into Aylesbury. There are 16 locks, falling some 95 feet to Aylesbury, and 19 bridges.

An information board by the first bridge shows some of the many species of duck that can be see on this stretch of the canal, especially in winter.

Alongside the canal just before the second road bridge (no. 17, built 1906) at Park Street can be seen part of the original 1870 factory of the Aylesbury Condensed Milk Company. By the 1880's it had become the Anglo-Swiss Condensed Milk Company, employing 150 workers and consuming 104,000 gallons of local milk monthly. It is now part of the Nestlé empire. The lock immediately beyond the bridge is no. 16 "Hills and Partridge", a name which refers to the proprietors of the now forlorn Walton water mill (probably 19th century, but on the site of an earlier mill), seen on the opposite bank ahead. About 200 yards beyond the lock is an access to a Tesco superstore, which houses a coffee shop.

Further along, and bordering the canal on the left for some distance, are the former works of BPC Hazells plc, one of the country's foremost printers and binders, who opened their factory here in 1867. The works closed in 1997 and are likely to be demolished and replaced by housing, resulting in a dramatic change to the landscape here!

In a further half a mile is bridge no. 15, the second of a long series of attractive brick arch structures that emphasise the narrowness of this canal. The adjacent lock, no 14 "Broughton", denotes the hamlet of the same name. In more open and pastoral countryside than we have seen so far, this a a popular spot with its recently built canal-side car park. An information board, just inside the car park, is worth consulting. From here on attractive views of the Chiltern Hills open up ahead and to the right.

Two miles further on, just before bridge no. 9 there is a small wharf on the opposite side. The bridge is followed by lock no. 12 "Red House". The Red House was once a pub but closed many years ago. This is an attractive spot suitable for rest and refreshment, as it once was for Aylesbury folk who reached here on their Sunday walks out of town.

In another mile, a boat restoration yard (usually with one or two interesting vessels under repair) is seen on the opposite bank just before bridge no. 7, which is followed by lock no. 11 "Puttenham Bottom", where there is a nicely restored lock cottage.

Walkers taking the shorter walk to Aston Clinton should leave the canal here, and follow the route instructions at the end of this chapter.

Bridge no. 4 (no number plate), in just over half a mile, has been restored. It is unique in the series for being of wooden construction and solely a footbridge. About 100 yards before the bridge, just to the right of the towpath, is a small iron marker denoting 1 mile from Marsworth Junction. On your route beyond lock no. 7 (unnamed) there are views ahead of Marsworth church tower, one of the chimneys of Pitstone cement works (due to be demolished), the chalk downland of Pitstone Hill (carrying the Ridgeway Path) and, further right, the wooded slopes of Aldbury Nowers.

In half a mile we go under bridge no. 1, then pass locks nos. 1 and 2, finally to reach the junction with the main Grand Union Canal, with British Waterways workshops to the left.

Continue along the towpath of the main canal (signposted "Brentford 39 ¼ miles"). There are always plenty of boats and visitors here.

The Grand Junction Canal, as it was originally, was built at the end of the 18th century to provide a short cut between Braunston, near Rugby, and Brentford on the River Thames west of London. Built to a new, wide standard, it very quickly became a busy and profitable trunk route, linking London with the industrial Midlands. Attempts to persuade other companies to widen their locks and establish a similar standard capable of carrying barges of 70 tons capacity were not, however, successful. The Grand Union Canal Company was the result of an amalgamation in 1929 of a number of companies.

Passing the seating area of the White Hart pub, you reach the road bridge carrying the B489.

The canal just below the bridge is often seething with enormous carp.

Go up to the bridge and cross the road carefully (traffic is controlled here by lights). To end the walk here and return to Aylesbury by bus, walk 40 yards along to the right to the bus stop. Otherwise, continue along the towpath of the main canal, passing lock no. 39 and the recently restored lock cottage. Stay with the canal as it bends left, passing below firstly Startops End and then Marsworth reservoirs to the right.

The reservoirs are interesting and attractive in their own right, with abundant wildfowl and other water birds. There are a number of information boards, and a leaflet describing walks around the reservoirs is available from a machine in the car park.

We now pass six sets of locks in quick succession, finally to reach lock no. 45, Marsworth Top Lock, at Bulbourne. We are now, at 430 feet, at the summit level of the Grand Union Canal. The Wendover Arm joins the main canal on the right, completing its 6 ¾ mile journey from Wendover.

To join the Wendover Arm, cross over the junction footbridge and double back underneath it to pick up the towpath, noting the map board on the bridge wall at the junction.

The principal purpose of the Wendover Arm was to act as a feeder to supply water to the summit of the main canal. The main source of that water was to be the diverted flow from the Well Head at Wendover. Shortly after construction began in 1793, it was realised that, at very little extra cost, the waterway could be built to carry boats, linking Wendover and the Vale of Aylesbury with principal markets throughout the country. However, the canal was built on porous chalk, which had to be puddled to prevent leakage. These measures were singularly unsuccessful, and leaks were the main cause of the canal's failure and ultimate closure. Attempts were made to stop the leaks, including drainage and partial relining in 1803 and 1856, but they failed to deal with the problem. Throughout the 19th century it continued to leak, causing great difficulties for traders and financial strains for the canal company. By 1894 it was actually taking water from the main canal, and by the turn of the century water losses were colossal. The canal struggled on for a few more years but inevitably abandonment came, in 1904. The stop lock was built at Tringford to prevent further drainage losses, and it is this top section, from Tringford to the junction at Bulbourne that has remained in water and navigable today. However, it retains a great deal of charm and interest, and improvements to the towpath in recent years have ensured its popularity with walkers and nature lovers. Indeed, a campaign at the time of writing to restore the whole canal to navigation has brought opposition from environmentalists and parish councils.

In half a mile, at the brick arch bridge at New Mill, it is necessary to leave the towpath by crossing a stile, then go up onto the narrow bridge (where traffic vies for the right of way!) and cross it very carefully to rejoin the towpath, now on the other side. The bank side here is dominated by the buildings of Heygates Mill.

Beyond the mill area, the Tring feeder enters on that bank. This stretch plays host annually to a colourful boating festival which raises funds for the Wendover Arms Trust.

Arrival in a few hundred yards at Tringford Pumping Station signals the abrupt end of navigation. It was built to pump water up from the neighbouring reservoirs to feed the summit level of the main canal via the arm. Once powered by powerful beam engines, it now houses electric motors which do the same job.

Cross over beyond the lock and continue ahead, to go up steps to a road over the now filled-in canal. Ignore the path opposite, turn right along the road and follow it very carefully, past the farm buildings and cottages of Little Tring to a public footpath signposted on the left, a distance of some 300 yards. Leave the road and go up a track for about 50 yards to meet the end of a hedge. Do not go straight on into a field, but fork right to cross a stile by a white metal gate, to rejoin the towpath, now flanking a visible but dry canal bed. Continue ahead along a very pleasant stretch, full of wildlife interest, and soon with fine views over Wilstone Reservoir to the right.

The reservoir, built to supply water to the Grand Union Canal, is now also a nature reserve, very popular with bird watchers.

In another mile, go under the cement-rendered brick arch bridge at the pretty hamlet of Drayton Beauchamp. Continue ahead now with trees over-arching the canal bed.

200 yards past the bridge a waymarked footpath leaves the towpath on the right, going up steps to afford a visit to the 15th century church, which has a number of interesting features. The monument to Lord Newhaven and his widow has been called "the best church monument in England"; there are some fine 14th century brasses in the chancel, and a wonderful east window depicting ten of the twelve apostles. *A note in the porch indicates where the key may obtained.*

Suddenly, soon after the church is passed, the canal is back in water, much narrower and shallower than before, but beautifully clear. On reaching Buckland Wharf in another half a mile, cross the extremely busy A41 with great care and rejoin the towpath, now on the opposite bank.

From here right through to Wendover, the towpath has been surfaced in recent years as part of a major refurbishment scheme, including information boards and promotional signs, featuring a kingfisher, quite a common sight along this stretch. The high wooded Chiltern escarpment is now quite close to the left, but the canal, as expected, keeps to the level by contouring around it. Green Park, formerly the site of a Rothschild property (Aston Clinton Manor, since demolished), but now a flourishing Bucks County Council conference and adult education centre, is to the right, immediately beyond the next bridge at Stablebridge Road.

On a now more wooded path, you arrive shortly at a brick wharf on the opposite bank, probably built to enable deliveries to be made to Aston Clinton Manor. To the left of the towpath here is an area of excavations known as Cobblers Pits, through which ran an old road, truncated by the building of the canal. An information board tells you more about the pits.

In another quarter of a mile go under Harelane Bridge, before passing a sculptured seating area and continue past RAF Halton's sports ground on the left and their airfield buildings on the right. Nearby, but out of sight and not open to the public, Halton House is a spectacular mansion in the style of a French Chateau for Baron Alfred de Rothschild in 1884. It now serves as the officers' mess for RAF Halton. The next bridge is of splendid ironwork, complete with the Rothschild monogram picked out in gold paint.

Shortly afterwards, you reach the road and flattened bridge at Halton village. It is worth a short detour along the road to the right to view the charming pictorial decorations on some of the houses close by.

Carefully cross the road and rejoin the towpath on the opposite bank.

The next bridge is another pleasant ironwork one. You soon then reach "The Wides" a low-lying wetland area with a variety of interesting wildlife and a "winding hole", where there is another informative noticeboard. The next information board is at a point where a branch railway which served Halton House crossed the canal A new wooden bridge now allows pedestrians access to the east bank, but our route continues ahead.

Finally we reach the southern terminus at the appropriately named Wharf Road, Wendover, where the water disappears under the bridge. Turn right along Wharf Road to reach the A413 (Aylesbury Road).

Across the road and along to the right can be glimpsed the top of a windmill tower. This was built in 1804. At 66ft in height and with two pairs of Derbyshire grit millstones, it was one of the largest windmills to be built in England. It is now a private house, but a public footpath goes beside it.

Turn right for the nearest bus stops (on the other side of the road for Aylesbury). To visit Wendover or to reach the station, turn left along Aylesbury Road, cross just before the mini-roundabout at the clock tower (which now houses the tourist information centre), and follow the main road as it bends right. For the station, continue past shops, cross Dobbin Lane, and go ahead along Pound Street for a short distance to reach the Shoulder of Mutton Inn on the right. Here turn right and down Station Approach.

Shorter walk

Walkers should follow the main walk from Aylesbury to bridge no. 7. Immediately before the bridge leave the towpath and go through a wooden swing gate up onto the road. Turn right, and in 50 yards leave the road at a small parking area on the right. Just beyond a metal "Aylesbury Ring" signpost, cross a footbridge, turn left and follow the twisting left-hand hedge for about 200 yards to a stile in the field corner. Here cross the stile, then go diagonally right across a large field, aiming for a point in the distant hedge ahead some 50 yards left of where it angles away sharply to the left. (Do not go around the boundary of this field – the right of way is diagonally across!). Here find and cross a footbridge and stile. Now turn sharp right to follow the right-hand fence, ditch and hedge all the way to a stile in the furthest corner. Cross the stile and continue to follow the right-hand hedge as it bends around the next field, until on reaching a line of tall trees, look out for and cross a pair of stiles and footbridge on the right. Now keep ahead across a meadow to a stile in the hedge ahead. Cross, and go slightly left over another meadow and the houses of Buckland village, with its church tower now visible on the right. Cross another stile and follow the grass track round to the left, passing a wooden barrier to reach an Aylesbury Ring signpost at a road (Peggs Lane). Turn right along the road, passing attractive cottages and the church entrance gate to the right.

On reaching a road junction, turn left, and with care follow this road, passing Manor Farm on the left and Nields Farm on the right to reach a crossroads in 250 yards. Here turn right along the pavement of the B489 Lower Icknield Way, passing 30 mph and Aston Clinton signs to reach the Rising Sun pub and the A41 at the east end of Aston Clinton village. Very carefully cross this busy road to the bus shelter opposite for westbound return buses to Aylesbury.

WALK 12: TRING STATION TO LEIGHTON BUZZARD

This walk starts in Hertfordshire and finishes in Bedfordshire, but for almost all its length is in Buckinghamshire. The first part follows the Ridgeway national trail for its last four miles to Ivinghoe Beacon (and here it really is a ridgeway – perhaps the finest on the Chilterns). Descending steeply from the beacon (with an alternative gentler descent) it then follows the Two Ridges Link through farmland and along the Grand Union Canal.

12 miles

Travel

Tring and Leighton Buzzard stations are on the main line from Euston to Milton Keynes and on to the Midlands. Frequent stopping trains connect both stations directly with Euston, Harrow, Watford, Berkhamsted, Bletchley and Milton Keynes. Tring station is two miles from Tring itself. There is a useful bus service from Aylesbury to Leighton Buzzard.

Refreshments

There are pubs at Tring Station, Ivinghoe Aston and Slapton, although the Carpenter's Arms at Slapton is closed Saturday lunchtimes and doesn't serve food on Sundays. A quarter-mile diversion will take you to the inn at Northall as an alternative. There is a canal-side pub just as you reach Leighton Buzzard; most of the other pubs and cafes are in the opposite direction to the station. It's also possible to get refreshments from the Tesco superstore beside the canal, and in the station (but not on Sundays).

Route

The London and Birmingham Railway, opened in 1838, was the first trunk railway, not just in Britain, but in the world. The journey initially used to take six and a half hours, half the time taken by the stagecoaches. Tring cutting, north of the station, was one of major engineering feats of the Victorian period.

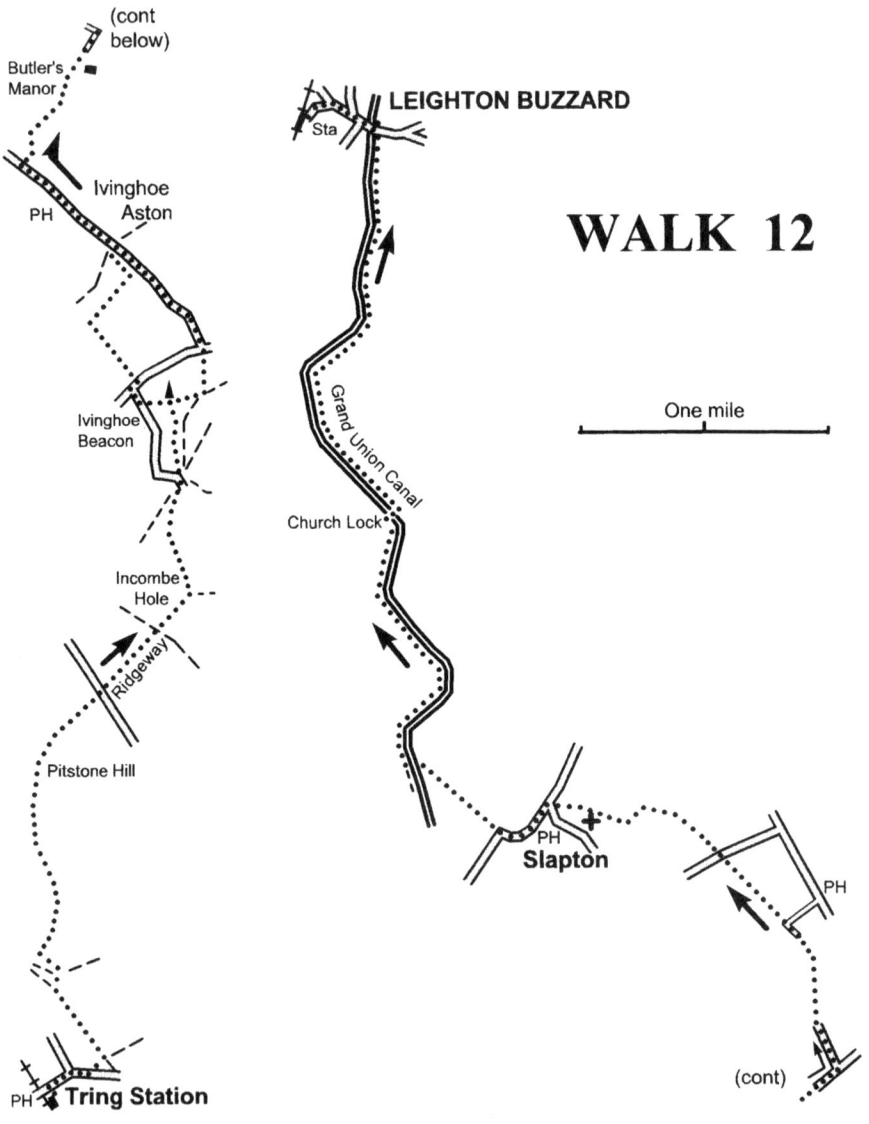

WALK 12

One mile

On leaving the station, turn right. Ignore the first junction on the left (Northfield Road), bear left in a further 100 yards and follow a Ridgeway signpost along a farm track. When this bears left go straight on. In another 100 yards go through a gate and turn left along a bridleway. After nearly half a mile take the footpath which bears right and climbs up the hill beside Duchie's Piece, a nature reserve and Site of Special Scientific Interest.

A board to the left of the path gives information about the reserve.

The path is well waymarked with Ridgeway acorn symbols as it winds its way up through the woods, soon passing another part of the nature reserve.

Further on you can see something of the devastation caused by the great storm of 1987. The trees here caught the full force of the gale, but natural regeneration is slowly taking place.

The Ridgeway path finally emerges through a kissing gate onto the open hillside. Follow the clear path as it gradually climbs towards the crest of the hill, bearing right to follow a ditch on the right.

This is a section of Grim's Ditch, the boundary ditch which features in Walk 7.

Eventually you will find yourself on the ridge of Pitstone Hill, with extensive views in most directions.

Regrettably, the view to the left was dominated, at the time of writing by the disused Pitstone cement works. An application to use the quarries in the foreground as a landfill site over 19 years was rejected following a public inquiry. As we went to press, the future of the site was uncertain; it would be nice to think that by the time you read this the view will be unspoilt.

In front, and to the right of, the cement works is Pitstone church, no longer in use, and no longer surrounded by its village. Further to the right, standing in the middle of a field, is the Pitstone windmill. This an early type of post mill, where the whole mill is turned by means of the "tail pole" to face the wind. The date 1627 carved on one of the timbers makes it probably the oldest in Britain. It was offered to the National Trust in 1937, and subsequently restored. *Open summer Sunday afternoons.*

Behind, and just to the right of the windmill, is Ivinghoe village. This was a market town once, but has declined over the centuries.

Sir Walter Scott is reputed to have taken the name of his most famous novel *Ivanhoe* from the village (or perhaps the beacon).

In the other direction, over to the right, is the wooded Ashridge Estate, in the care of the National Trust, and a favourite area for walks and picnics. Just above the trees can be seen the top of the monument erected in 1832 to the 3rd Duke of Bridgewater, the "Canal Duke". *Open afternoons except Friday, April to October.*

Continue along the crest, with the fence to your right, bearing slightly right with the fence. After a short descent, our route goes over the flank of the hill ahead, leaving the fence further to the right. Continue straight ahead, making for a stile by a car park, where there is an information board about Pitstone Hill and the chalk grassland which it typifies.

Cross the car park and the road, go through a kissing gate and follow the Ridgeway path, which is still signposted, along a track between two open fields. Continue straight ahead at the next kissing gate up the open hillside, and follow the path as it goes around the head of the dramatically steep valley of Incombe Hole.

On reaching a stile and a gate, don't cross the stile, but keep to the left, leaving the fence on your right. Go through a copse, and after another 100 yards with the fence on your right, go through a kissing gate, and follow the Ridgeway path over some open hillside and down to a road. Cross the road, with care, take the left-hand fork gently uphill and follow the well-used path up onto the ridge. In less than half a mile you will reach the summit at Ivinghoe Beacon, and the end of the Ridgeway long distance path.

Just below the steepest part of the climb to the summit, a shallow ditch winds round to the left; this marks the boundary of an early Iron Age hillfort. Around the summit there are traces of Bronze Age round barrows marking burial sites.

The view from the summit is stunning. Below, and slightly to the left, the nearest village is Ivinghoe Aston, which we shall soon be walking through. Beyond, and also on our walk, is the village and church of Slapton. Beyond that is our destination – Leighton Buzzard. Further left, on a low wooded hill, can be seen Mentmore Towers, the extraordinary mansion built by Sir Joseph Paxton, architect of the Crystal Palace, for Baron Mayer Amshel de Rothschild. Across to the right, on an outlying ridge of the Chilterns, is the famous White Lion of Whipsnade, carved out of the chalk below Whipsnade Zoo.

From the Ordnance Survey trig point, go left at right-angles to your previous direction. Aim for the left-hand end of a short fence and go straight down this very steep hillside, making for a point just to the left of a cattle-grid, clearly visible on the road below. *If you feel this is too steep, an alternative route is described at the end of this chapter.*

On the way down, pass the left-hand end of another short length of fence, and on reaching the road turn right. In 100 yards is a T-junction at a main road. Cross this very carefully, walk along a very short distance to the right, and take the Two Ridges Link on the left. Our route follows this all the way to Leighton Buzzard from here, and most of it is waymarked, but not always with "Two Ridges" signs. Walk along the left-hand edge of the field, though a kissing gate and ahead along the edge of the next field. At the field corner turn right and follow the fence to the far end where you will find a kissing gate on the left. Go through this and walk along the side of the field with the hedge and road on your right. At the field corner, go through a kissing gate on your right to join a road. Follow the road through Ivinghoe Aston for half a mile.

300 yards past the end of the 40 mph limit, take a footpath on the right over a stile, following a track on the left of the hedge towards some farm buildings. On reaching the farm our route bears off to the left, through a gate, over a bridge, across an old orchard (look for a waymark post) to a stile into a field corner.

The orchard was once part of a large concentration here devoted to the growing of a small damson-like plum called the "Aylesbury Prune".

Continue along the edge of the next field. At the end of the field cross two stiles, and go almost straight ahead, making for a large willow tree. At the end of this field, cross a bridge between gates. Carry on across the next field in the same direction, passing the moated Butler's Manor on the right, to a gateway and cattle grid leading to a made-up lane ahead.

After 150 yards, take another surfaced lane to the left. Follow this as it eventually becomes a grassy track. When the track peters out into a path, follow it along the edge of a field, cross a stile and another field, then another stile, followed by a gate. This leads to an enclosed path with a stream on the left. In a short distance it crosses the stream and continues on the other side. The path becomes a metalled track, then a lane.

To reach the pub at Northall, follow the lane when it turns right. Facing you at the end, and across the main road, is the Northall

Inn. To rejoin the walk after your refreshment stop, simply retrace your steps.

Carry on in the same direction as the way, at first a concrete track, becomes a grassy path, then a track again, to reach a road. Cross this and continue in the same direction beside a large field with a ditch and a hedge on your right. At the end of the field, go diagonally to the left across the next field to a waymark post at a stream crossing, and on to another waymark post and a bridge. Follow the hedge on the left across the next field, turn right at the field corner, and in 100 yards go left through a gap in the hedge, and over a stile. Bear right to cross the field making for a stile halfway along the fence, then to another stile to the left of a row of new houses, followed shortly by a futher stile which leads onto a road. Turn left and walk along the road through Slapton, passing the timber-framed Carpenter's Arms and the Old Book Shop on the left.

At the end of the village follow the road round to the right at a junction, and where the road then turns left go straight ahead over a stile and along a track. In a quarter of a mile the track ends at a gate and a stile. Cross the stile and carry straight on, following the path as it curves to the left to cross a bridge over the Grand Union Canal. Cross a stile immediately on the right to follow the towpath on the left bank. Directions for the three miles from here to Leighton Buzzard are unnecessary – simply follow the towpath, which changes sides after the first mile at Church Lock.

Something of the history of the canal is given in Walk 11. The tiny 14th century Grove parish church was restored in 1888 and has been converted into a private house.

Arriving at Leighton Buzzard, go under a road bridge and turn sharp right up a ramp to Leighton Road, turn right and cross the canal.

To reach the station, bear left in 100 yards to along to go along Old Road, and in another 200 yards bear left again (still Old Road). At the next junction, turn left down Station Road, which, not surprisingly, leads shortly to Leighton Buzzard station.

Alternative descent from Ivinghoe Beacon

On reaching the Ordnance Survey trig point, turn right and follow the crest of the hill to a stile in 250 yards. Cross this, and after a few yards bear left and head towards a waymark post at the edge of a hawthorn copse. Take the path which descends the hill between the trees and straight across the open space beyond to a stile. Cross this and go ahead through another small area of woodland, ignoring a crossing path, to emerge at a main road. Cross the road, very carefully, go down the road opposite, and in half a mile, at the beginning of Ivinghoe Aston, the main route joins from the left.

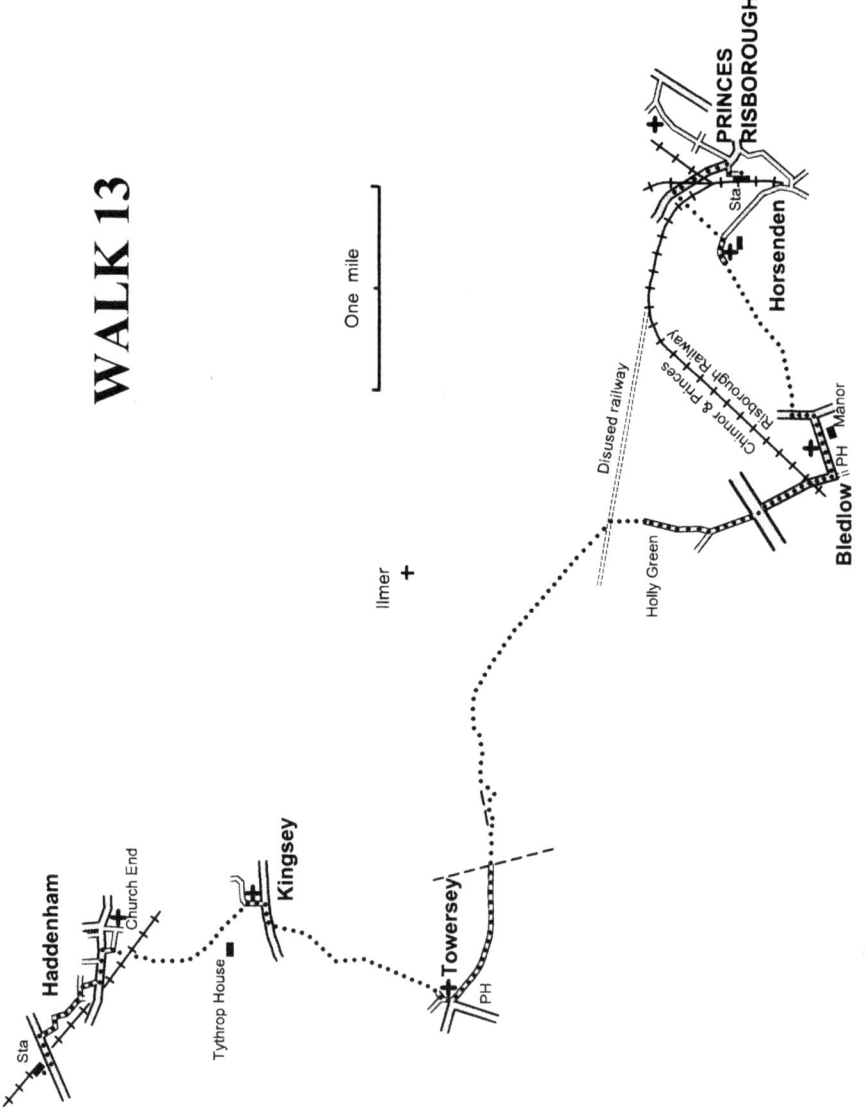

WALK 13

One mile

Haddenham

Church End

Sta

Tythrop House

Kingsey

Towersey

PH

Ilmer

Disused railway

Holly Green

Chinnor & Princes Risborough Railway

Bledlow

Manor

PH

PRINCES RISBOROUGH

Sta

Horsenden

WALK 13: HADDENHAM TO PRINCES RISBOROUGH

An easy walk through open countryside on the edge of the Vale of Aylesbury, passing through, as most walks in this area do, some attractive villages, and with the Chilterns seldom out of sight as a backdrop. The middle section can be muddy in winter.

9 miles

Travel

Haddenham and Thame, and Princes Risborough stations are both on the Chiltern Line from Marylebone and High Wycombe to Bicester, Banbury and the Midlands. Princes Risborough is linked to Aylesbury by bus and train, and there is a good bus service to Haddenham from Aylesbury and Oxford. Bus travellers should alight at Haddenham Church End and turn right opposite the church to go down Flint Street and pick up the walk where the road bends.

Refreshments

There are pubs at Haddenham, Towersey and Princes Risborough, but the Lions of Bledlow is nicely situated and also at a good strategic point on the walk.

Route

The walk starts at Haddenham and Thame Parkway station. As you leave the station, turn left, and after 150 yards turn right down Sheerstock.

Even the walls of this housing estate are in imitation of "witchert" walls which are such a feature of Haddenham and other nearby villages (see Walk 14).

Follow the road as it twists and turns, becoming Slave Hill and then Whitecross Road, and ignoring cul-de-sacs until you reach a T-junction. Turn left, and after 300 yards turn right down Flint Street.

Flint Street used to be called Duck Street; the name was changed because of the smell associated with the raising of ducks in

cottage back yards. If you have never explored Haddenham it is worth at least taking a slight detour to Church End by continuing along Flint Street at this point to the pond, church and the cluster of attractive old houses. See Walk 14 for more about Haddenham.

At the first bend, in 100 yards, take a footpath off to the right between witchert walls. The path soon bends to the left, goes through a gateway followed by a kissing gate, across a small field and bears right to go under a railway bridge. As the track bears round to the right, go slightly left through a kissing gate and follow the path with the hedge on your right. Pass a large pond on your left, and then, as the hedge bears slightly right go straight ahead across the the corner of the field to a gate and a stile. In 200 yards cross a stream by a wooden bridge, go through a belt of trees and over another bridge and a stile. Ignore a path to the right, and take the cross-field path ahead. As you go up the gentle slope a wide view opens up across to the Chilterns escarpment on the left. Continue with the metal fence and drive on the right. Over your left shoulder at this point you get a good view of Haddenham Church End.

To the right is Tythrop House. This dates back to the 17th century and was built in its present form for James Herbert, sixth son of the Earl of Pembroke. After many vicissitudes, it was restored in modern times.

At the corner of the field go through a kissing gate to reach the drive. Cross the drive and go down a track on the right. At the end turn right along the road through the small village of Kingsey, with the church on the left.

The parish of Kingsey used to be in Buckinghamshire, was transferred to Oxfordshire in 1894, and as a result of a swap with neighbouring Towersey, moved back to Bucks in 1939. The small church was built in 1892/93 in an old fashioned style, using the stone from the previous church. *Not normally open.*

At the main road, cross with great care, turn right to walk along the wide verge, cross a drive which diverges into two, cross a ditch and take a track (bridleway sign), also on the left. Follow the bridleway sign as our route bears right, then at a concrete bridge bear slightly left to join a track alongside the original one. Continue along the track with the hedge on the left and a barbed wire fence on the right. The track becomes eventually a narrower enclosed path, which at length becomes a gravel drive, then a lane. At a road junction turn left, with the duckpond, then the Old Vicarage on the right, and Towersey parish church on the left.

We are now, for a mile or so, in Oxfordshire. The church is 15th century, with a more recent tower. *A note in the porch says where the key may be obtained.*

Towersey is renowned for the major international folk festival which is held here in September. It started in the 1970's, as a way of raising money for a new village hall, and has grown considerably over the years.

At the crossroads, turn left (signposted "village only") along Manor Road, passing Towersey Manor on the left. The road soon leaves the village and enters open country. At a "crossroads" in three quarters of a mile, go straight ahead, following the signposted bridleway, soon an enclosed path between hedges. After 300 yards the way fords a stream, but a bridge is provided for walkers.

From here to the far corner of the large field on the left, the route described is not the official right-of-way. The correct route goes through a gate on the left and crosses the field to another gate in the far corner, passing just to the left of a fence corner after 200 yards. Follow the fenced path ahead as it twists and bends along the left-hand bank of the stream at the edge of a large field. At the corner of the field, the path turns to the left, to leave the stream, and then in 200 yards, at the next corner of the field, bears right to become a wider way between trees. In nearly half a mile go through a gate into a large open field. The view opens out here, with remote Ilmer and its church tower to the left, and the Chilterns ahead and over to the right.

The stream now rejoins our route on the right. Follow the bank for 100 yards or so to a footbridge, cross this, and continue roughly in the same direction, now with the stream on the left. At the end of the field you will find a stile in the hedge, followed immediately by a footbridge and another stile. Emerging from the hedge, continue to the far end of this long field, making for a point near the middle of the further hedge. Go through a waymarked gap in the hedge, and bear left to cross the next field to another stile by a five-bar gate. Continue ahead across the next field, through the gap in the hedge, and through the next long field in the same direction. Cross a stile at the far end, and walk across the track bed of the disused Princes Risborough to Oxford branch railway.

Follow the path as it bears left and then right to go round a small lake. Cross a stile, then bear slightly right, heading for a white cottage. Go through a kissing gate and turn left to go down Holly Green Lane. At the next road junction go straight ahead and in another quarter of a mile cross Chinnor Road very carefully, and go down West Lane nearly opposite. In quarter of a mile the lane goes under the now partially restored Chinnor and Princes Risborough Railway, to reach the Lions of Bledlow public house.

The line was opened in 1872 as a branch of the Great Western Railway from Princes Risborough to Watlington. It closed to passenger traffic in 1957, but remained open for freight until 1989 to serve the Chinnor cement works. Four miles of the line have been restored, and steam hauled trains are operated from Chinnor on most weekends from Easter until the end of October.

Turn left at the small green in front of the pub to walk through the centre of this delightful village.

The church of Holy Trinity, in a very spacious graveyard, has a number of interesting features including an Aylesbury type Norman font and some fragments of wall paintings. *Usually open on summer Saturday and Sunday afternoons.*

In a short distance, on the left, is a gate leading into the Lyde Garden, which is not to be missed. It's an intriguing and tranquil water garden laid out, with great ingenuity, in a steep ravine. *Freely open every day.*

Opposite is Bledlow Manor, dating from the 17th and early 18th centuries. It has been the family home of the Carringtons since 1800, the present owner being Lord Carrington, the former statesman. The garden, which can only be glimpsed from outside, is described in the Good Gardens Guide as "an elegant English garden of exceptional quality". *The garden is open by written appointment from May to September, and occasionally for charity.*

At the end of the village street, turn left, and in 150 yards take a signposted footpath on the right. Ignore the drive to the right after 100 yards, cross a stile by a gate, go past a house, through another gate and into a yard with an interesting collection of old ploughs. Cross a stile into the field ahead. A stretch of the Chilterns escarpment is ahead, dominated by Whiteleaf Cross.

This distinctive landmark carved out of the chalk, with its pyramidal base, has been the subject of much debate. It was said by tradition to commemorate a victory by the Saxons over the Danes. It was first described by Francis Wise in 1742, and he claimed, too, that its origins go back to Saxon times. More cautious recent writers suggest the 17th century. There is a smaller chalk cross above Bledlow, but this is not easily visible from our route.

96

Continue straight ahead, with the hedge on the right, to another stile, then along the side of the next field. At the next stile, turn left for 70 yards along an enclosed path, then right to follow the left-hand edge of a large field. At the end of this field, carry straight on to cross a further field, then go through a hedge, over a small stream and cross a stile. Go over the next field, passing a tennis court and barn, to cross a stile by a five bar gate, and emerge into a lane at the hamlet of Horsenden.

The church is only the chancel of the previous medieval building, and was restored in 1855. *It is not generally open.* A former Rector is said to have invented aspirin, curing his parishionners' aches and pains with extract of willow bark. The nearby manor house was built in 1810 on the site of the former house owned by Sir John Denham, the 17th century poet. There are still the remnants of a moat and fishponds in the grounds: the stream which fed them flows under the lane a little way past the church.

Go along the lane, with the church to the right, for 200 yards. Just past Gate Cottage, take a gravel track on the left. Cross a stile in 50 yards, and another at the further end of the farmyard. Continue ahead in the same direction, to come to the end of a road through a small industrial estate with a railway bridge straight ahead. Go under the bridge, to reach a main road (Summerleys Road) and turn right. At a railway bridge, cross with care to the footway on the other side of the road. Go under the next bridge with great care, as the footway almost disappears. 300 yards further on, cross the road and go down Station Approach on the right to reach Princes Risborough station.

Although considerably built up, Princes Risborough retains its unspoilt town centre. To reach it, go past the Station Approach and walk down the next road on the left – Manor Park Avenue. This becomes a private road, but a public footpath goes along it. At the end it leads into Church Street. Here is the stately parish church of St Mary's *(usually open 10.00 to 12.00 and 2.00 to 4.00)*, and just beyond, the 17th century redbrick manor house *(National Trust, but only open Wednesday afternoons by appointment)*. Church Street leads to the equally attractive High Street. At the corner of both is the Market Square, and the small Market House, built in 1824, with arches below and the Town Council chamber above.

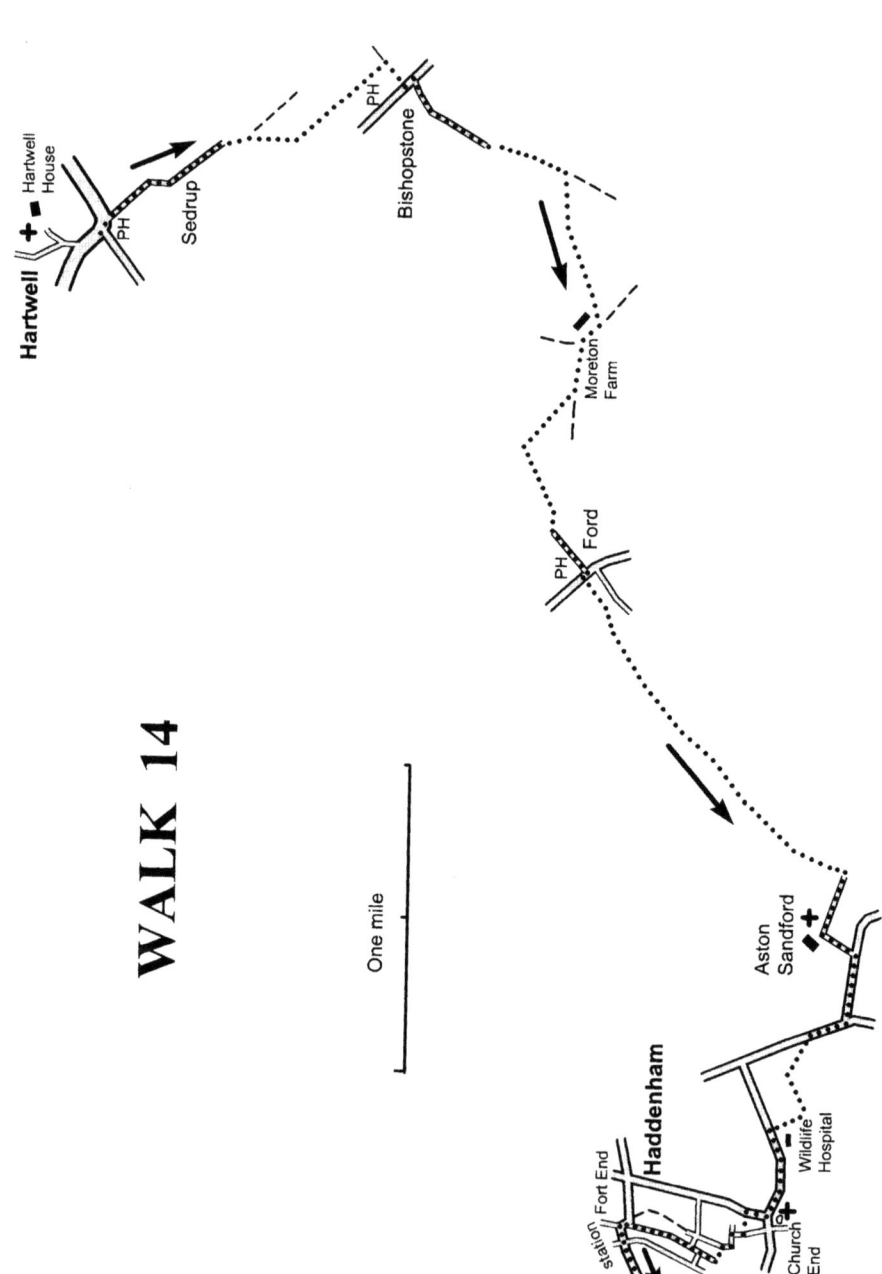

WALK 14

One mile

WALK 14: HARTWELL TO HADDENHAM

A walk across open and generally level country with distant views
of the Chiltern Hills. As is often the case in the Vale of Aylesbury,
you may find the going in places rough at some times of the year,
either muddy, overgrown or both! It's a rewarding walk, however,
with wonderfully open scenery, the unspoilt hamlet of Ford
marking the halfway point. The walk ends at the old village centre
of Haddenham, passing the idyllic setting of Church End Green
and going between ancient "witchert" walls.

7 miles

Travel

*Hartwell and Haddenham are both served by a frequent bus service from
Aylesbury to Thame and Oxford, although less frequent on Sundays. Aylesbury is
on the Chiltern Line to Marylebone via Amersham or High Wycombe, and
Haddenham is on the line from Marylebone and High Wycombe to Banbury and
Birmingham.*

Refreshments

*There is a pub at the start of the walk, one close by the route at Bishopstone,
another at Ford (closed on Mondays), and a choice of them at Haddenham.*

Route

Alight from the bus at the Bugle Horn public house, Hartwell.

Behind the wall on the other side of the main road is Hartwell
House. Even the wall itself is interesting, as it has huge fossil
ammonites built into it. The house has a fascinating history. It was
built for the Hampden and Lee families in the 16th and 18th
centuries. From 1809 to 1814 it was the home of Louis XVIII, exiled
King of France and his family. When he returned to reclaim the
throne, he laid out an English Garden at Versailles, modelled on
that of Hartwell. It subsequently became the home of Ernest Cook,
heir to Thomas Cook of tourism fame, then a finishing school and

secretarial college. In more recent years it was lovingly restored at great expense and converted into a hotel and restaurant. A meal, or even coffee, here gives an opportunity to experience what the house was like in its heyday. Many of the rooms are as they were in the 18th century. The main hall features a Jacobean staircase, with 24 carved figures surmounting the balusters, including more recent additions such as Sir Winston Churchill and GK Chesterton. There is a striking equestrian statue of Frederick, Prince of Wales, outside the main entrance.

By the main drive to Hartwell House is the 18th century Gothic church of St Mary's, now, sadly, just a shell. It was apparently built in imitation of the chapter house of York Minster, and was the first of a number of octagonal churches built in England. The architect was Henry Keene, who also built the Guildhall at High Wycombe.

Take Sedrup Lane on the left-hand side of the pub. This forms part of the North Bucks Way long distance path. Soon the Chiltern escarpment can be seen stretched out on the horizon ahead, and in almost half a mile the hamlet of Sedrup is reached, an attractive cluster of mostly thatched cottages. Bear right on the bridleway, passing the small green on the left to follow the track which shortly enters an arable field. Here leave the North Bucks Way and go half right across the field. On reaching the far corner continue ahead with the hedge on the right. At the end of the field cross a stile by a metal gate, and continue in the same direction, crossing a further stile, until reaching a junction with the North Bucks Way at a wide track. Here turn right and in 200 yards emerge onto the road at Bishopstone.

The Harrow public house is about 100 yards to the right. Our route turns left with the North Bucks Way and very soon, opposite the war memorial, turns right down Moreton Lane. After passing through a gate with a stile beside it, the lane becomes a rough track, which crosses a bridge to enter a field. Follow the right-hand hedge to a wooden gate at the end of the field. Here leave the North Bucks Way again, to strike out half right across a large field, heading 100 yards to the left of a house on the skyline, converted from a barn which was all that was left of Moreton Farm. Go right, through a gate with a Swans Way waymark.

Swans Way is a long distance bridle route, which runs 65 miles from Salcey Forest, on the Northamptonshire border, to Goring on the River Thames.

Ignore a bridle gate on the right (where Swan's Way leaves us again) and continue, to follow a wire fence on the right. As the path nears a hedge make for a stile by the gate ahead. Cross the stile, and in the next field bear left to a gate about two thirds of the way up its length. Bear slightly right across the next field (following the middle one of three waymarked paths) to a stile on the other side, about 100 yards to the left of a barn. Continue in the same direction across another field to a gate. Once on a track, head in the same direction to a metal gate, passing the moat of Moat Farm, to arrive at the hamlet of Ford. Follow the track, now metalled, through Ford, passing the Dinton Hermit pub.

The pub is named after John Biggs, Secretary to Simon Mayne (one of those who signed Charles I's death warrant) and, it was rumoured, possibly one of the masked executioners of the king. After the death of his patron, he lapsed into melancholy and remorse. He lived for 36 years in an old hut at nearby Dinton, without ever changing his clothes and living on what local people gave him.

At a road junction, turn right, then almost immediately left over a stile at a footpath sign. Go ahead, parallel with the cottages on the other side of the hedge. After a double stile head to the right of the first black barn, followed by a barn with crumbling witchert walls.

Witchert is a stiff, white clay-like substance found locally. It used to be mixed with chopped straw and water and layered onto a foundation of stone or brick. It was sometimes subsequently rendered with lime mortar. There are many examples of its survival in the area, particularly in Haddenham, and it was used for barns, houses and boundary walls. Its use is characterised by irregular rounded corners.

Cross over a stile just before another black barn. Cross a farm track, go through a metal gate, and head slightly right to another metal gate in the hedge ahead. Once through this, follow the left-hand hedge for two fields. After a footbridge, head slightly right to a clump of willow trees and cross another footbridge. Cross the next field to another stile, then continue ahead in the same direction with the hedge on your left, for the next four fields. After crossing a stile, and with the buildings of Aston Sandford immediately ahead, turn left into the field on your left, then bear right passing a house on the right. In front of a metal gate bear right again, to go over a stile by another metal gate and follow the lane ahead through Aston Sandford.

The church was drastically rebuilt and restored in 1877, but retains a small green and yellow stained glass figure of Christ in the east window. *A note in the porch says where the key may be obtained.* **Just beyond is the Manor House, one of the few domestic buildings designed by Sir George Gilbert Scott – "The greatest architect of the Gothic revival", and architect of St Pancras Station and the Albert Memorial. The fact that his grandfather, Thomas Scott, had been Rector here might have something to do with it! In fact, Thomas Scott, who is buried in the churchyard here, was famous in his own right for his biblical Commentary, described by a contemporary as "the greatest theological performance of our age and country".**

At the church follow the road round to the left, and at the road junction turn right for 150 yards, being very careful of the traffic. At the next road junction, turn right and walk for a further 300 yards until you see a signpost in the left-hand hedge. Cross the stile here, and then bear right across the field in the direction shown by the sign.

The route has now picked up the Church Farm Trail which we will follow to Haddenham. This is a County Council initiative intended "to give an insight into how farming, wildlife and recreation can live together in harmony".

Do not cross the stile next to the metal gate, but turn left in front of it. Cross a tree-planted area by stiles, follow round a small pond and turn right over a footbridge. Turn slightly left to another stile and go ahead, passing through a picnic area with the farm buildings on the right and St Tiggywinkles wildlife hospital on the left.

St Tiggywinkles takes its name from the specialist hedgehog treatment unit opened in 1985. The present building, opened in 1991, is the world's first wildlife teaching hospital, dealing with some 15,000 animal and bird casualties a year.

At the entrance turn left into Haddenham, being careful of the traffic, reaching Church End Green in 400 yards.

The large pond which dominates Church End would, in past times, have been swarming with white Aylesbury ducks, for duck

breeding was a big cottage industry in Haddenham. Every day the drakes, each followed by his harem of six to eight ducks would be led to the pond by their owners. The duck eggs were hatched by hens, and those destined for the table (which was most of them) only ever got one swim – when they were half-grown – "to feather properly".

The parish church of St Mary is largely 13th century. The Norman font is of the "Aylesbury" type found in 22 churches, including (as well as Aylesbury), Bledlow, Great Kimble and Great and Little Missenden. This one is carved with monsters. The other buildings around the green are of different periods, but blend harmoniously together. The oldest is probably the 15th century Church Farm House, to the left of the church.

Haddenham experienced extensive growth in the post-war years, but the core of the village remains little changed. The last half mile of this walk gives you a taste of that old village centre, with its alleyways lined with witchert walls, a High Street with no shops and little traffic which starts from a "dead-end", and a variety of cottages of various styles and periods. You will see that most of the witchert walls are now topped with tiles, rather than the original thatch, and that many are rendered.

Walk up Churchway opposite the pond. Just past the Green Dragon, take a narrow alleyway, with the delightful name of Dragon Tail. At the end, at the tiny Skittles Green, turn right, then left at a junction into The Croft. After the road bends right, take a walled alleyway on the left (no name, but with a "No Cycling" sign and opposite no. 8A). This leads to the bottom of the High Street. Walk all the way up to emerge at the main road through the village at Fort End. Buses for Oxford stop here; those for Aylesbury on the other side, a little to the left. Haddenham and Thame Station is half a mile to the left along the main road (which becomes Thame Road).

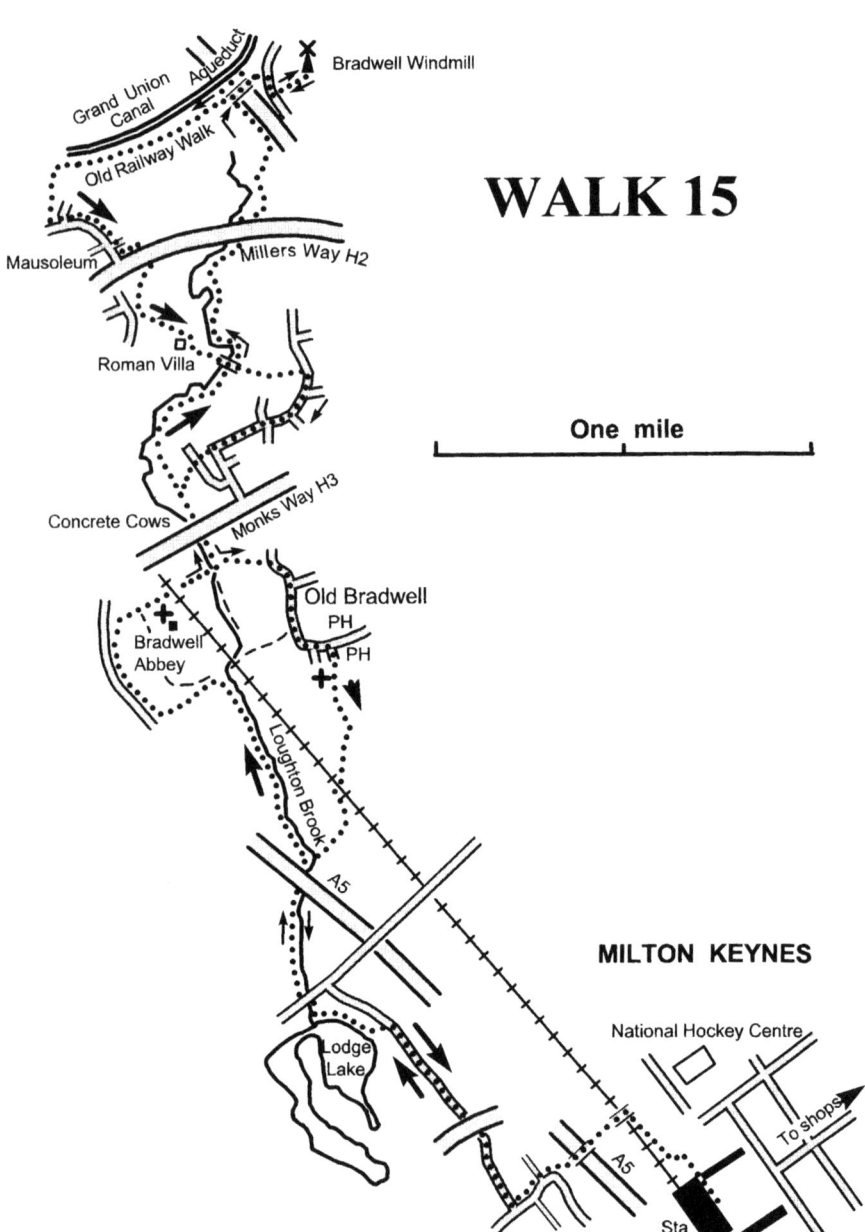

WALK 15

One mile

MILTON KEYNES

WALK 15: LOUGHTON VALLEY, MILTON KEYNES

Unlike the others in this book, this is not a linear walk, or even a circular walk. It follows a figure-of-eight course through attractive parkland and carefully preserved countryside, passing the famous concrete cows, an historic abbey, a windmill, a canal aqueduct and a Roman villa. It's all on hard-surfaced "redways" and "leisure routes", part of Milton Keynes' unique cycle and pedestrian system.

7 miles

The OS Pathfinder maps are of little help on this walk. If you feel you need a map we recommend the Official City Map at a scale of 1:10000, published by the New Towns Commission, or the smaller scale Redway Guide.

Travel

Milton Keynes is on the main railway line between Euston and Birmingham, which also serves Harrow, Watford, Hemel Hempstead, Berkhamsted and Northampton, among other places. It is at the hub of a network of bus services, with good services from Aylesbury, Leighton Buzzard, Bedford, Cambridge and Northampton.

Refreshments

Refreshments are available at the station. The main shopping centre is a mile up Midsummer Boulevard, opposite the station, with many eating places there and between the station and the centre. There are two pubs in Vicarage Road, Bradwell Village.

Route

We have included Milton Keynes in this book, because, although it became a new "unitary authority" in 1997, it is still historically and geographically a part of Buckinghamshire.

Milton Keynes was planned as Britain's first new city; it was intended to be, and is, much larger than any previous new town. The site was first announced in 1966. The government "selected the name of a tiny village engulfed by the new city, because the three old towns due for absorption (Bletchley, Wolverton and Stony Stratford) all seemed touchy about local pride".

From the start it was the intention to preserve the integrity of the towns and villages within Milton Keynes, to retain something of a rural landscape between the settlements, and to create "linear parks" which would follow natural features such as rivers. Loughton Valley is an example of such a park.

It was argued that it would be impossible to plan a city satisfactorily for 100% car use, and various revolutionary layouts and transport schemes were considered, including a monorail system. In the end, the city finished up with a basic grid pattern and conventional public transport. The redways, described as "Britain's largest urban footway/cycling network", were named when a secretary accidentally typed "redway" instead of "pedway" which was the name originally intended.

Turn left out of Milton Keynes Station, soon passing the entrance to Phoenix House on the right. Continue ahead until you reach a grassy bank. Turn left, then follow the footpath as it turns right.

The National Hockey Stadium is across to the right. This was opened in 1996 as the official home of the English Hockey Association, and has an artificial pitch.

Bear left to cross the bridge over the railway, then over the dual-carriageway A5. Continue on the redway, with its red tarmac, passing some new housing on your right. 200 yards after crossing the bridge, turn right along Bradwell Road. After going under a road bridge and passing a Guide Centre on the left and the National Badminton Centre on the right, follow the left-hand pavement as it leaves the road and goes down to Lodge Lake.

Continue, with the lake on your left. Just before a weir, turn right and go under a road bridge. Cross a red bridge and immediately turn right. On the right is Loughton Brook which we shall walk beside, on and off, for nearly two miles. After going under a concrete road bridge (the A5 again), fork left.

The riding track to our left is part of Swan's Way, the long distance bridleroute which runs the whole length of Buckinghamshire.

After about a third of a mile, turn sharp left onto a redway (leaving the brook, which we rejoin later). Follow this, ignoring junctions to left and right, as it curves around to the right, to go alongside a road bordering an industrial estate. 30 yards before a power line, soon after the chapel of Bradwell Abbey becomes visible away to the right, turn right to follow another redway (signposted Youth Hostel), which goes past the entrance to the Abbey grounds.

Bradwell Abbey was a Benedictine priory, founded in 1154. It fell into disrepair even before the dissolution of the monasteries. It was eventually replaced by a farm, which utilised some of the building material. The only significant part to survive is the small 14th century Chapel of Our Lady of Bradwell, which contains some important wall paintings of the period. Also on the site is the City Discovery Centre, established to promote a wider understanding and appreciation of the history and development of Milton Keynes. It includes an interpretation centre, library, lecture theatre and cafeteria. *The centre is mainly open for organised educational visits. The chapel is only open for guided tours, but the centre plans to allow inspection of the wall paintings by remote TV camera.*

The redway goes under the railway line.

The first turning left immediately before a bridge (the bridleway along the bank of the stream) gives a five minute detour to visit the famous concrete cows. Probably one of the best known outdoor works of art in the country, the cows were designed in 1978 by Liz Leyh, then Artist in Residence for Milton Keynes, and given by her to the city. Other sculptures are to found elsewhere on the redway network.

The redway then crosses the bridge to a cross-junction of paths. Turn left here, to take another redway which goes under H3 Monks Way. Away to the left, on the other side of the brook are the famous concrete cows

Fork left in 70 yards to leave the redway and follow a path as it meanders through the valley, with the brook on your left. Ignoring turnings on the left, pass beneath a wooden bridge. Follow the path as it goes over a smaller bridge and sharp left, and then curves gently right, still beside the brook. At a cross-junction continue ahead and pass under H2 Millers Way. Over the next quarter of a mile, the path gradually diverges from the brook and rises gently to go parallel to a main road and under a bridge. Follow the path as it loops up to the left, and go over the bridge you have just gone under.

On reaching a road in 50 yards, turn right and take a path on the left to visit Bradwell Windmill.

A plaque gives the history of the windmill and explains about its construction. *It is not normally open to the public.* This is the furthest point on the walk, and a good spot for a picnic.

Retrace your steps to the road, turn right and follow the paths down to the canal bank. Walk alongside the canal as it crosses the aqueduct.

This is the Grand Union Canal, described in some detail on Walk 11. The aqueduct was built in 1991, surely the most recent in Britain.

At the end of the railings, turn sharp left, and then right to follow a redway.

This section is known as the Old Railway Walk, and it follows the line of the former Wolverton to Newport Pagnell branch line.

After a third of a mile, follow the redway as it bears left uphill and under an arch between two buildings. In another 100 yards turn left at a small children's playground onto another redway which curves to the right alongside a road. Just before another arch through a building, you will see a grassy mound away to the right.

This is the site of a Roman mausoleum. Information is available from a plaque on the site.

After going under the arch, turn left, and in a further 100 yards go under a road bridge on the right, up the slope, and turn left opposite a shop. Bear immediately right, through the car park, left again and down to the right and the site of Bancroft Roman Villa.

At the lower end of this large site, whose plan can be seen on the ground, are three information plaques give detailed plans and reconstructions of the complex as it was.

On leaving the villa, take the redway to the left which heads towards the long footbridge at the bottom of the valley, and cross the Loughton Brook and our earlier route. Continue up and round a play area. Turn right at a road (signposted Bradwell). Continue – still on the redway – along this road, passing several side roads and the end of Octavian Drive, across a minor road, then downhill, past the concrete cows again, and back under H3 Monks Way. Take the first redway on the left (opposite the bridge you crossed on your outward walk). Go to the top of the playing field and turn right along the road at the top (Abbey Road).

We are now in Old Bradwell – one of the villages absorbed by the new city, but still retaining much of a village atmosphere.

Turn down the second road on the left (Vicarage Road), then right to pass the youth hostel on the right.

100 yards beyond the turning for the youth hostel are two pubs.

Continue through the churchyard.

The church of St Lawrence is the parish church for Bradwell. It has been much restored, but has two of the oldest bells in Buckinghamshire. *It is normally locked.*

Turn right in front of houses and follow the footpath to a bridge over the railway. Cross this, and when you come to a T-junction of paths, turn left, following signs to Lodge Lake. From here it's a question of retracing your steps: through the A5 underpass, over the red footbridge, under the road bridge to bring you back to the lake. Follow this round, along Bradwell Road, over the A5, over the railway, turn right, left and right, and continue to the station.

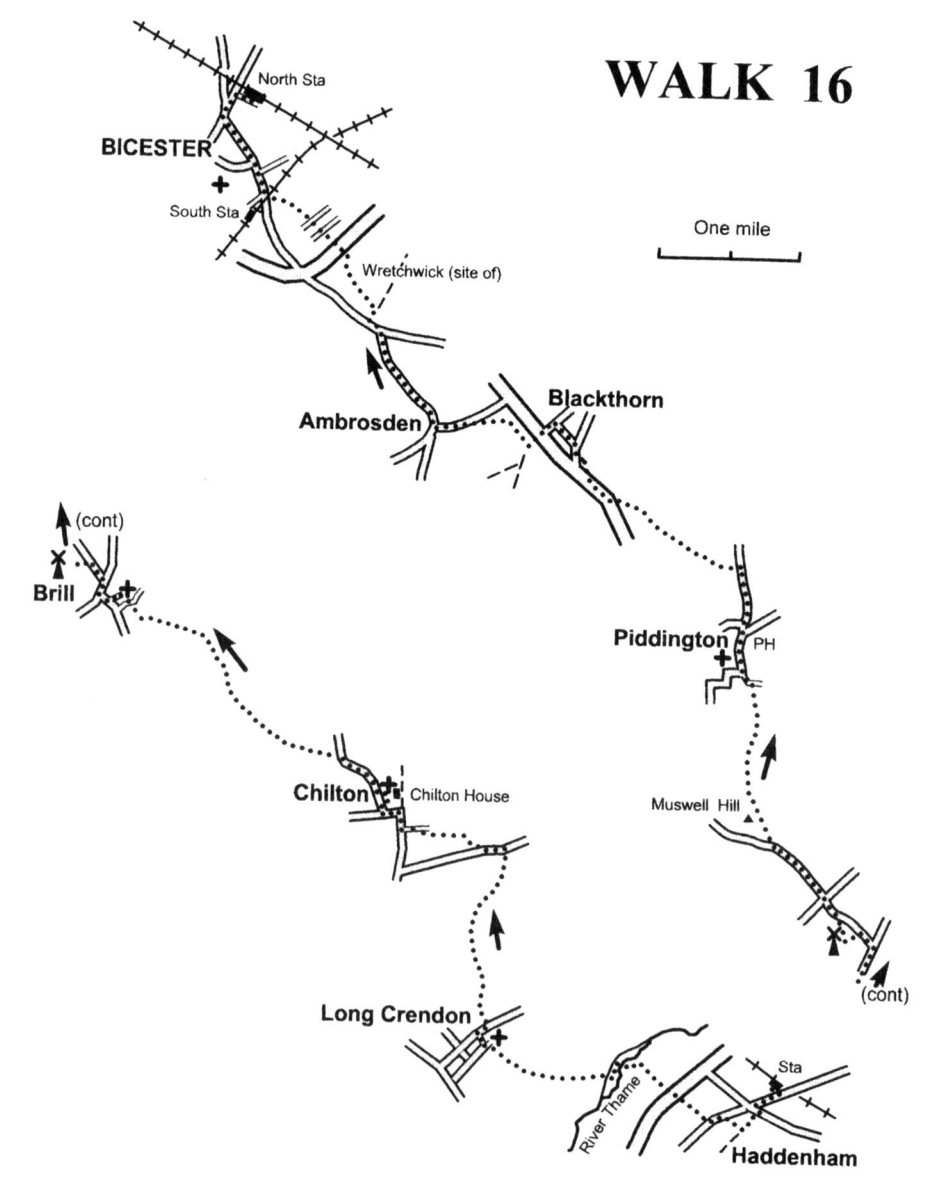

WALK 16

North Sta

BICESTER

South Sta

Wretchwick (site of)

One mile

Ambrosden

Blackthorn

(cont)

Brill

Piddington PH

Chilton Chilton House

Muswell Hill

(cont)

Long Crendon

River Thame

Sta

Haddenham

WALK 16: HADDENHAM TO BICESTER

We have saved this challenge walk for the end of the book. It's fairly tough going, much of the area is little walked and you are likely to find more path problems than usual, especially after you cross the border into Oxfordshire. However, it has its rewards. The villages it passes through are interesting and attractive, and the countryside mostly unspoilt, with outstanding views from a number of hilltops on the way.

17 miles

Travel

Haddenham and Thame Parkway station and Bicester North station are both on the Chiltern Line between Marylebone, High Wycombe and the Midlands. Haddenham has a good bus service from Oxford and Aylesbury. Bicester Town station has a weekday service to Oxford, and there are frequent buses between Bicester and Oxford.

Refreshments

There are pubs in Long Crendon, Brill (we don't usually recommend particular pubs, but the Pheasant, overlooking the windmill, is particularly good, and nearly half way), Piddington (open at lunchtimes on Saturday and Sunday only), and, of course, Bicester. Note that the "PH" marked on OS maps at Blackthorn no longer exists. Bicester is also well supplied with cafés and restaurants

Route

On leaving Haddenham and Thame Parkway station, turn right, to walk along the verge of this busy road for a quarter of a mile, Then cross very carefully, take the road opposite and almost immediately turn right onto a bridleway. In 250 yards take a footpath right at a path crossing, returning diagonally to the road, aiming for where a stream emerges from under the road. Cross the road again and walk along to the left for 200 yards. Take a footpath on the right heading towards the second electricity pole to the left of the tallest tree. Cross the very busy A 418 with great care. Take the track ahead downhill. Where the track bears right near a clump of trees, continue ahead along the field edge to a stile, then go diagonally across the field to a footbridge over the River Thame.

Once over the river turn left, and in 150 yards turn right to cross the millstream to a stile ahead. From here to Long Crendon our route follows the Thame Valley Walk.

This is a 15 mile waymarked walk developed by Aylesbury Vale District Council with the help of the Aylesbury and District Group of the Ramblers' Association, based on a walk devised by Peter and Diana Gulland for our previous publication *The Vale of Aylesbury Walker.*

Walk diagonally left across the field. At the field corner cross a stile and a footbridge and continue along the edge of the next three fields, following the hedge as it bends to the right. At the end of the third and largest field go through a gate on the right, and then immediately bear left towards a white gate at the far corner of the field. Continue between fences to emerge onto a drive, which ends soon at crossroads, with Long Crendon church on the right, and the Courthouse over the road.

The Courthouse dates from the 14th century, and was probably first used as a wool store. The manorial courts were held here from the time of Henry V until recent times, with accommodation for the poor on the ground floor. *The upper floor is open from April to September: Wednesday afternoons, Saturday, Sunday and bank holiday Mondays 11am to 6pm.* **The imposing parish church, with a magnificent 16th century east window and fine monuments, is** unfortunately *not generally open to the public.*

The High Street, which winds away to the left, has a wonderful collection of old houses, many thatched. Nikolaus Pevsner, in *The Buildings of England: Buckinghamshire,* **states that there are more medieval houses of cruck construction, that is using pairs of curved timbers, in this village than almost anywhere else in England. From about 1560 until the industrial revolution, Long Crendon was a major centre of needle making as a cottage industry, many of the cottages having large windows to give extra light.**

Go straight ahead, soon to reach a T-junction. Turn right here, and 70 yards past the end of the speed limit, cross the road to a footpath, initially in a sunken hollow way. At a stile in 100 yards, bear half right across a field aiming for a stile with a long barn behind. Cross the stile, a footbridge and another stile into a farmyard, turn left to follow waymarks around the end of the large barn to another stile, and join a track coming from the right. Turn left onto the track and follow this for the next half a mile. After crossing a stile by a gate, bear right down a dip to another stile by a gate. Cross the next field to a further stile. Once over this, cross to the hedge 20 yards ahead and turn right, following the hedge as it bends right, then left. Some 350 yards after entering the field, at a slight kink in the hedge, cross a stile on the left partly hidden by foliage. Continue with the hedge now on your right to a double stile and a bridge in the corner of the field. Go diagonally left across the next field, making for the brow of the hill, then around the outside of the perimeter fence of Wombwells Farm to another stile in the field corner, to emerge at a road. Turn left here to follow the road uphill.

In 200 yards, where the road curves left, take a footpath on the right (over an old gate – the sign was hidden in foliage when we walked the route). Cross the field diagonally left, aiming for a bend in the opposite hedge near a cedar tree, with a long barn behind. Bear left to follow the hedge to the field corner, cross a stile and in another 150 yards cross another stile by a metal gate to join a lane by a farm entrance. Turn right at a T-junction to follow the road through the village of Chilton. Where the road turns left, it's worth following the footpath along the drive straight ahead for a short distance for a view of Chilton House, then returning to the road.

The house was rebuilt for Lord Chief Justice Carter in 1740, and was based on a "reduced model" of the then Buckingham House, later to become Buckingham Palace. The palace subsequently had a new facade added in 1913, so they no longer look similar. Note the ha-ha on the right of the drive, the concealed drop which kept the animals in the parkland without interrupting the splendid view from the house.

Follow the main road as it bends to the right in 100 yards (signposted Dorton), and take the path through the churchyard, passing the church itself.

The church has a number of interesting features. If you go to the south-east corner of the churchyard and look up at the east wall of the nave, you will see a stone effigy of a knight in chain mail – an unusual position for such a monument. In the east wall of the churchyard are two doorways connecting the church with the manor house; the 15th century original (now blocked up) and a later one from the 17th century. Inside are many monuments to the

Croke family who were Lords of the Manor from 1529 to 1682. One of them was Speaker of the House of Commons at the time of Elizabeth I; another – Sir George – was one of the two judges who gave judgement against Charles I in the ship money case against John Hampden. There is an imposing memorial to Lord Chief Justice Carter. The two war memorials show another, sadder, way in which Chilton was touched by history. You will see that the eighteen men who lost their lives in the First World War came from only eleven families. It is claimed that Chilton sent the highest proportion of its men as volunteers to the front, of any town or village in England.

Continue along the path through the churchyard, to emerge though a gate, and turn right up the road. Follow the road as it curves left, then, at the right-hand bend, take the second footpath on the left through a kissing gate, bearing diagonally right across this small field to a stile. Almost immediately cross another stile and aim for a point 100 yards from the left hand corner of the field. Cross a stile behind a willow tree here and continue ahead in the same direction, aiming just to the right of the hedge-line ahead. Cross a bridge and a stile. Aim slightly right across the next field to a stile into a strip of woodland (not shown on the OS map). Go ahead through the woodland to the next stile.

In the next field, do not take the path that may or may not be marked out straight ahead, but turn right along the field edge for a few yards then bear left across the field, aiming towards the middle of Chiltonpark Farm on the top of the hill. This is a right of way, though it wasn't visible on the ground when we walked it. Cross two stiles and a ditch and aim for the lowest point in the line of trees ahead, slightly to the left of the farm. Go through the copse, then bear slightly right up the steep slope, aiming just to the right of the brick barns. As you near the buildings, cross a stile. Go round the right-hand side of the farm buildings to an old gate, then bear right to follow the ridge, aiming for a stile and a gate just to the left of a pair of electricity poles.

In the woodland down to the right is the site of an ill-fated scheme to establish a spa to rival those of Bath and Leamington. A pump room was built in 1834, and the spa, based on the evil smelling sulphurous liquid issuing from the chalybeate spring, was successful for a short time. In the end it was defeated by the remoteness of the site, and little now remains to be seen. Further to the right is the impressive Dorton House, built for Sir John Dormer in 1675. It is now a school.

Bear left, aiming for the highest part of the field. Cross a stile and carry on in the same direction, aiming about 100 yards to the right of a large clump of tree, to a stile in the field corner between two gates. Continue in the next field with the fence on your right. Go over the next stile and turn right. Continue through a gate, along a path across the valley head to a stile between houses. Turn left to follow a road across a small green. After 100 yards take the tarmac footpath which bears right to pass the churchyard.

The church of All Saints may once have been a royal chapel, as Edward the Confessor had a palace nearby. The church is entered through a Norman doorway, but was extensively restored in late Victorian times.

At the end of the path, continue along a road for a short distance, and bear right at the end.

Brill is like no other village in Buckinghamshire, partly because of its hilltop position, partly because it is, as described by Sir John Betjeman, "a redbrick decayed Georgian and 17th century town". It was described in 1622 as "a town well graced with many fair houses and good buildings, and the best yeomen of any town in the shire, delicately situated upon a fertile, fruitful hill... and the earth within serving for the best brick and all earthen vessels....". Brill was an important centre for clay-based industries from the 13th to the 19th century, including bricks, tiles and pottery.

Turn right onto Church Street, past the Red Lion. Bear right at the war memorial (signposted Ludgershall). In 200 yards turn left at the Sun into Windmill Street. The Pheasant public house is on the left just before the common, and overlooking the windmill.

Bear left to visit the windmill.

Brill windmill is a good example of a post mill, and the surviving one of three on the common. Built in the 1680's, it is one of the oldest in the country. Just before it, on the right, is an information board explaining its workings. *Open on Sunday afternoons, April to September.* The pits and mounds in this area are the remnants of the clay diggings for the former pottery industry.

It is hard to imagine, looking at the predominantly rural outlook from this hilltop, that Brill was once the farthest flung outpost of the London Underground system. A horse tramway was built in

1871 by the local landowner, the Duke of Buckingham, to serve his estate at Wotton House. A year later, passengers were being carried by steam hauled trains, and the line extended to Brill Station, at the bottom of the hill, nearly a mile from the village centre. The line was later re-laid and a connection made to the main line at Quainton Road, and in 1899, it became, in effect, a branch of the Metropolitan Railway. It remained a rather eccentric and erratic line, with only four trains each way a day, until its closure in 1935.

From here, make your way over to the right, and down between the various hillocks, to rejoin the road further down. Go over the crossroads at the bottom of the hill, and follow the road ahead as it climbs the other side, using the verge wherever possible. After the Thames Water site on the left, ignore a stile with a permissive path on the right, and carry on uphill to the next gate on the right, almost at the top of the hill and half a mile from the crossroads. Take the stile by the gate and bear left, aiming perhaps 70 yards to the right of the Ordnance Survey trig point on the skyline.

This is Muswell Hill, described by Sir Arthur Bryant as "one of the noblest viewpoints in southern England". Because we are on a small plateau, we can see more of the further distance, with the Chilterns on the horizon behind us. Over to the right, some three miles away, is Wotton House. This was built in 1704 by a little known architect, John Keene, and was, like Chilton House, based on Buckingham House. After various fires and rebuildings, it became derelict, until its restoration in the late 1950's. The outstanding views of Oxfordshire and the Cotswolds do not reveal themselves until we shortly begin the descent on the other side of the hill.

Continue in the same direction, aiming for a stile towards the left hand end of a large clump of trees. As we reach the stile we enter Oxfordshire. Cross the stile and the drive ahead to a bridle gate slightly to your left. Go through the gate and turn right to follow the fence on the right, with the steep hillside on the left. The path becomes steeper, but still in the same general direction, with the fence on the right, and crossing two stiles on the way down. At the bottom of the hill cross a double stile, and continue in the same direction, along the side of a large field. At the end of the field cross another double stile, aiming just to the right of a house with four dormer windows. This will lead you to a stile by a gate.

The pattern of raised strips in this field are the "ridge and furrow" signs of the medieval method of ploughing. The ridges were produced by up-and-down ploughing of long, narrow strips of land, which threw the soil towards the centre of the strip, the strips being separated from each other by a double furrow. The subsequent conversion of the land to pasture fossilised the pattern.

Cross the stile and bear right, heading for a stile between a bungalow on the left and houses on the right. In a short distance go over a second stile to emerge in a lane. Turn left into Piddington. At the next junction go straight ahead passing the church on the left.

The church has a painting on the wall of St Christopher, which was discovered in 1933. On the west wall are remains of writings dated 1645. The poet John Drinkwater spent his childhood here, and asked to be buried in this peaceful spot. His grave is under a tree opposite the porch, the headstone inscribed with one of his poems: "In some new brain the sleeping dust will waken,
Courage and love that conquered and were done,
Called from a night by thought of man forsaken,
Will know again the gladness of the sun".

Carry on through the village, passing the Seven Stars pub on the right. Ignore a turning on the right (to Ludgershall). At the next junction bear right (signposted Aylesbury) and in nearly half a mile, opposite a roadside seat, turn left, onto an unmarked track, which soon runs alongside the boundary of an army depot. 100 yards after the fence of the depot begins, turn right, through an old kissing gate (at the time of writing the sign was hidden in the hedge).

The next mile was full of problems when we walked it – if you don't find barbed wire, overgrown hedges, electric fences and padlocked gates, it will be a pleasant surprise, and Oxfordshire County Council will have done its duty! Bear diagonally left across the field to twin gaps in the hedge (plastic over barbed wire "marks" the exit) and bear slightly right, aiming for a pylon, through an old hedge-line to a footbridge. After the bridge, turn left along the hedge to a gap in the field corner, cross a shallow ditch, and turn sharp right, past a pylon, and over an awkward footbridge into the next field. Cross diagonally left to the opposite corner with farm buildings beyond. Go through a gate, straight across the track, over the gate opposite, then directly across the field and over two gates. Now bear left, around farm buildings, and exit onto the farm drive.

Turn right onto a busy road towards Blackthorn, using the verge wherever possible. About 150 yards past the small bridge over the River Ray go through the small gate on the right and along the disused old road. After 200 yards rejoin a new road to walk along Thame Road (signposted Ambrosden), passing a junction on the right. Follow the road as it bears left on meeting Lower Road, to reach a T-junction with the busy B4011.

Cross the road with care, and take the bridleway opposite. Pass through another gate, and turn right at the fence corner. Cross two stiles and continue straight across the next field. Cross a footbridge and stile and turn left. Cross another footbridge and stile, and bear half right across the next field to yet another footbridge and stile. Continue in the same direction across the next field to join a road. Turn left along the road towards Ambrosden to a T-junction.

There used to be a large Roman camp at Ambrosden, and it has been suggested that it was named after Ambrosius Aurelianus, a Romano-British leader who fought the invading Saxons in the 5th century. Appropriately, Ambrosden is now surrounded by massive military camps.

Turn right (signposted Bicester), to walk along the footway on the right hand side, passing army housing estates on both sides, followed by Bicester Garrison buildings. On reaching the A41, turn left, using the traffic island, to walk along the footway on the left hand side.

Much of the A41 follows the line of Akeman Street, the Roman road from Verulamium (St Albans) to Cirencester. Where the present road bends to the right here, Akeman Street headed off to the left towards the Roman town of Alchester two miles away.

As you draw level with the first house on the right, cross this extremely busy road with great care, go through a metal gate and follow the track just to the right of the cottage. At the end of the first field, turn left to walk along the left-hand side of a large field. At the field corner cross two stiles with a plank bridge between them, to continue along the edge of an even larger field. Go through the gate at the end, then straight ahead across a farm track, to join another track which bends to the right and enters the farmyard of Middle Wretchwick Farm.

The shallow bumps and depressions in the field to your left indicate the site of the medieval hamlet of Wretchwick. It was owned by Bicester Priory, and in March 1489 all the inhabitants

were evicted so that the land could be turned over from arable to pasture, as the wool trade was very profitable at that time. Middle Wretchwick Farm was well named; it was indeed in the middle of Wretchwick, which extended on both sides.

Turn left to go down the left-hand side of some large barns, passing through three gates. At the end of the barns, bear right, then immediately left, to cross a stile and a busy road. On the other side of the road follow a tarmac cycle/footway through a housing estate, passing the end of a long pond on the right. Follow this path as it crosses an estate road. At a T-junction go left and almost immediately right onto another cycle/footway, passing a school on the right, crossing another estate road, and continuing in more or less the same direction to a abrupt dead-end. Cross the stile in the fence ahead and go half-left across a field to a bridge and a stile. Go straight across the next field to a gate, bear left across the field after that to a stile. Finally cross the last field diagonally to an inconspicuous stile in the field corner. A short enclosed path leads to a road at a level crossing.

Walk over the level crossing to follow the road to Bicester town centre. Bicester Town Station (for trains to Oxford) is down the first road on the left. Otherwise go straight ahead ignoring roads to left and right, to walk down the pedestrianised Sheep Street.

You will probably not have the energy by now to do much exploring of Bicester. The characterful Market Square, however, is just off to the left immediately before Sheep Street (*market day Friday*), and from there can be glimpsed the parish church, which has some impressive Norman arches and many monuments.

The bus station is down a passageway to the left off Sheep Street. To reach Bicester North Station (for the Chiltern Line), continue along Sheep Street, which becomes North Street, go ahead at a five-way junction, to walk along Buckingham Road. On reaching a railway bridge, turn right up Chiltern Approach to the station.

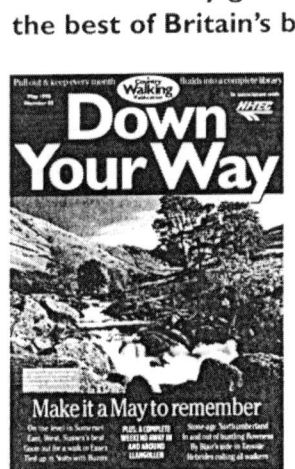